PHRASEBOOK

— CZECH —

By Andrey Taranov

THE MOST IMPORTANT PHRASES

This phrasebook contains
the most important
phrases and questions
for basic communication
Everything you need
to survive overseas

T&P BOOKS

Phrasebook + 3000-word dictionary

English-Czech phrasebook & topical vocabulary

By Andrey Taranov

The collection of "Everything Will Be Okay" travel phrasebooks published by T&P Books is designed for people traveling abroad for tourism and business. The phrasebooks contain what matters most - the essentials for basic communication. This is an indispensable set of phrases to "survive" while abroad.

This book also includes a small topical vocabulary that contains roughly 3,000 of the most frequently used words. Another section of the phrasebook provides a gastronomical dictionary that may help you order food at a restaurant or buy groceries at the store.

T&P Books Publishing
www.tpbooks.com

ISBN: 978-1-78492-452-2

This book is also available in E-book formats.
Please visit www.tpbooks.com or the major online bookstores.

FOREWORD

The collection of "Everything Will Be Okay" travel phrasebooks published by T&P Books is designed for people traveling abroad for tourism and business. The phrasebooks contain what matters most - the essentials for basic communication. This is an indispensable set of phrases to "survive" while abroad.

This phrasebook will help you in most cases where you need to ask something, get directions, find out how much something costs, etc. It can also resolve difficult communication situations where gestures just won't help.

This book contains a lot of phrases that have been grouped according to the most relevant topics. The edition also includes a small vocabulary that contains roughly 3,000 of the most frequently used words. Another section of the phrasebook provides a gastronomical dictionary that may help you order food at a restaurant or buy groceries at the store.

Take "Everything Will Be Okay" phrasebook with you on the road and you'll have an irreplaceable traveling companion who will help you find your way out of any situation and teach you to not fear speaking with foreigners.

TABLE OF CONTENTS

T&P Books Publishing

PRONUNCIATION

T&P phonetic alphabet	Czech example	English example
[a]	lavina [lavɪna]	shorter than in ask
[aː]	banán [banaːn]	calf, palm
[e]	beseda [bɛsɛda]	elm, medal
[ɛː]	chléb [xlɛːp]	longer than bed, fell
[ɪ]	Bible [bɪblɛ]	big, America
[iː]	chudý [xudiː]	feet, meter
[o]	epocha [ɛpoxa]	pod, John
[oː]	diagnóza [dɪagnoːza]	fall, bomb
[u]	dokument [dokumɛnt]	book
[uː]	chůva [xuːva]	pool, room
[b]	babička [babɪʧka]	baby, book
[ʦ]	celnice [ʦɛlnɪʦɛ]	cats, tsetse fly
[ʧ]	vlčák [vlʧaːk]	church, French
[x]	archeologie [arxɛologɪe]	as in Scots 'loch'
[d]	delfín [dɛlfiːn]	day, doctor
[dʲ]	Holanďan [holandʲan]	median, radio
[f]	atmosféra [atmosfɛːra]	face, food
[g]	galaxie [galaksɪe]	game, gold
[h]	knihovna [knɪhovna]	huge, hat
[j]	jídlo [jiːdlo]	yes, New York
[k]	zaplakat [zaplakat]	clock, kiss
[l]	chlapec [xlapɛʦ]	lace, people
[m]	modelář [modɛlaːrʃ]	magic, milk
[n]	imunita [ɪmunɪta]	name, normal
[nʲ]	báseň [baːsɛnʲ]	canyon, new
[ŋk]	vstupenka [vstupɛŋka]	bank, trunk
[p]	poločas [poloʧas]	pencil, private
[r]	senátor [sɛnaːtor]	rice, radio
[rʒ], [rʃ]	bouřka [bourʃka]	urgent, flash
[s]	svoboda [svoboda]	city, boss
[ʃ]	šiška [ʃɪʃka]	machine, shark
[t]	turista [turɪsta]	tourist, trip
[tʲ]	poušť [pouʃtʲ]	tune, student
[v]	veverka [vɛvɛrka]	very, river
[z]	zapomínat [zapomiːnat]	zebra, please
[ʒ]	ložisko [loʒɪsko]	forge, pleasure

LIST OF ABBREVIATIONS

English abbreviations

ab.	-	about
adj	-	adjective
adv	-	adverb
anim.	-	animate
as adj	-	attributive noun used as adjective
e.g.	-	for example
etc.	-	et cetera
fam.	-	familiar
fem.	-	feminine
form.	-	formal
inanim.	-	inanimate
masc.	-	masculine
math	-	mathematics
mil.	-	military
n	-	noun
pl	-	plural
pron.	-	pronoun
sb	-	somebody
sing.	-	singular
sth	-	something
v aux	-	auxiliary verb
vi	-	intransitive verb
vi, vt	-	intransitive, transitive verb
vt	-	transitive verb

Czech abbreviations

ž	-	feminine noun
ž mn	-	feminine plural
m	-	masculine noun
m mn	-	masculine plural
m, ž	-	masculine, feminine
mn	-	plural
s	-	neuter
s mn	-	neuter plural

CZECH
PHRASEBOOK

This section contains
important phrases that may
come in handy in various
real-life situations.
The phrasebook will help
you ask for directions, clarify
a price, buy tickets, and
order food at a restaurant

T&P Books Publishing

PHRASEBOOK CONTENTS

T&P Books Publishing

The bare minimum

Excuse me, ...	**Promiňte, ...** [promɪnˈtɛ, ...]
Hello.	**Dobrý den.** [dobriː dɛn]
Thank you.	**Děkuji.** [dekujɪ]
Good bye.	**Na shledanou.** [na sxlɛdanou]
Yes.	**Ano.** [ano]
No.	**Ne.** [nɛ]
I don't know.	**Nevím.** [nɛviːm]
Where? | Where to? | When?	**Kde? | Kam? | Kdy?** [gdɛ? | kam? | gdɪ?]

I need ...	**Potřebuju ...** [potrʒɛbuju ...]
I want ...	**Chci ...** [xtsɪ ...]
Do you have ...?	**Máte ...?** [maːtɛ ...?]
Is there a ... here?	**Je tady ...?** [jɛ tadɪ ...?]
May I ...?	**Můžu ...?** [muːʒu ...?]
..., please (polite request)	**..., prosím** [..., prosiːm]

I'm looking for ...	**Hledám ...** [hlɛdaːm ...]
the restroom	**toaletu** [toalɛtu]
an ATM	**bankomat** [baŋkomat]
a pharmacy (drugstore)	**lékárnu** [lɛːkaːrnu]
a hospital	**nemocnici** [nɛmotsnɪtsɪ]
the police station	**policejní stanici** [polɪtsɛjniː stanɪtsɪ]
the subway	**metro** [mɛtro]

a taxi	**taxík** [taksi:k]
the train station	**vlakové nádraží** [vlakovɛ: na:draʒi:]

My name is …	**Jmenuju se …** [jmɛnuju sɛ …]
What's your name?	**Jak se jmenujete?** [jak sɛ jmɛnujɛtɛ?]
Could you please help me?	**Můžete mi prosím pomoct?** [muːʒetɛ mɪ prosiːm pomotst?]
I've got a problem.	**Mám problém.** [maːm problɛːm]
I don't feel well.	**Necítím se dobře.** [nɛtsiːtiːm sɛ dobrʒɛ]
Call an ambulance!	**Zavolejte sanitku!** [zavolɛjtɛ sanɪtku!]
May I make a call?	**Můžu si zavolat?** [muːʒu sɪ zavolat?]

I'm sorry.	**Omlouvám se.** [omlouvaːm sɛ]
You're welcome.	**Není zač.** [nɛni: zatʃ]

I, me	**Já** [jaː]
you (inform.)	**ty** [tɪ]
he	**on** [on]
she	**ona** [ona]
they (masc.)	**oni** [onɪ]
they (fem.)	**ony** [onɪ]
we	**my** [mɪ]
you (pl)	**vy** [vɪ]
you (sg, form.)	**vy** [vɪ]

ENTRANCE	**VCHOD** [vxot]
EXIT	**VÝCHOD** [vi:xot]
OUT OF ORDER	**MIMO PROVOZ** [mɪmo provos]
CLOSED	**ZAVŘENO** [zavrʒɛno]

OPEN	**OTEVŘENO**
	[otɛvrʒɛno]
FOR WOMEN	**ŽENY**
	[ʒenɪ]
FOR MEN	**MUŽI**
	[muʒɪ]

Questions

Where?	**Kde?** [gdɛ?]
Where to?	**Kam?** [kam?]
Where from?	**Odkud?** [otkut?]
Why?	**Proč?** [protʃ?]
For what reason?	**Z jakého důvodu?** [z jakɛ:ho du:vodu?]
When?	**Kde?** [gdɛ?]

How long?	**Jak dlouho?** [jak dlouho?]
At what time?	**V kolik hodin?** [v kolɪk hodɪn?]
How much?	**Kolik?** [kolɪk?]
Do you have ...?	**Máte ...?** [ma:tɛ ...?]
Where is ...?	**Kde je ...?** [gdɛ jɛ ...?]

What time is it?	**Kolik je hodin?** [kolɪk jɛ hodɪn?]
May I make a call?	**Můžu si zavolat?** [mu:ʒu sɪ zavolat?]
Who's there?	**Kdo je tam?** [gdo jɛ tam?]
Can I smoke here?	**Můžu tady kouřit?** [mu:ʒu tadɪ kourʒɪt?]
May I ...?	**Můžu ...?** [mu:ʒu ...?]

Needs

I'd like …	**Rád /Ráda/ bych …** [raːd /raːda/ bɪx …]
I don't want …	**Nechci …** [nɛxtsɪ …]
I'm thirsty.	**Mám žízeň.** [maːm ʒiːzɛnʲ]
I want to sleep.	**Chce se mi spát.** [xtsɛ sɛ mɪ spaːt]

I want …	**Chci …** [xtsɪ …]
to wash up	**se umýt** [sɛ umiːt]
to brush my teeth	**si vyčistit zuby** [sɪ vɪtʃɪstɪt zubɪ]
to rest a while	**si chvilku odpočinout** [sɪ xvɪlku otpotʃɪnout]
to change my clothes	**se převléknout** [sɛ prʒɛvlɛːknout]

to go back to the hotel	**se vrátit do hotelu** [sɛ vraːtɪt do hotɛlu]
to buy …	**si koupit …** [sɪ koupɪt …]
to go to …	**jít do …** [jiːt do …]
to visit …	**navštívit …** [navʃtiːvɪt …]
to meet with …	**se setkat s …** [sɛ sɛtkat s …]
to make a call	**si zavolat** [sɪ zavolat]

I'm tired.	**Jsem unavený /unavená/.** [jsɛm unavɛni: /unavɛna:/]
We are tired.	**Jsme unavení /unaveny/.** [jsmɛ unavɛni: /unavɛnɪ/]
I'm cold.	**Je mi zima.** [jɛ mɪ zɪma]
I'm hot.	**Je mi horko.** [jɛ mɪ horko]
I'm OK.	**Jsem v pořádku.** [jsɛm v porʒa:tku]

I need to make a call.

Potřebuju si zavolat.
[potrʒɛbuju sɪ zavolat]

I need to go to the restroom.

Potřebuju jít na toaletu.
[potrʒɛbuju jiːt na toalɛtu]

I have to go.

Musím už jít.
[musiːm uʒ jiːt]

I have to go now.

Teď už musím jít.
[tɛtʲ uʒ musiːm jiːt]

Asking for directions

Excuse me, ...	**Promiňte, ...** [promɪnⁱtɛ, ...]
Where is ...?	**Kde je ...?** [gdɛ jɛ ...?]
Which way is ...?	**Kudy ...?** [kudɪ ...?]
Could you help me, please?	**Můžete mi prosím pomoct?** [muːʒɛtɛ mɪ prosiːm pomotst?]

I'm looking for ...	**Hledám ...** [hlɛdaːm ...]
I'm looking for the exit.	**Hledám východ.** [hlɛdaːm viːxot]
I'm going to ...	**Jdu ...** [jdu ...]
Am I going the right way to ...?	**Jdu správným směrem do ...?** [jdu spraːvniːm smnerɛm do ...?]

Is it far?	**Je to daleko?** [jɛ to dalɛko?]
Can I get there on foot?	**Dostanu se tam pěšky?** [dostanu sɛ tam peʃkɪ?]
Can you show me on the map?	**Můžete mi to ukázat na mapě?** [muːʒɛtɛ mɪ to ukaːzat na mape?]
Show me where we are right now.	**Ukažte mi, kde právě teď jsme.** [ukaʃtɛ mɪ, gdɛ praːve tɛdⁱ jsmɛ]

Here	**Tady** [tadɪ]
There	**Tam** [tam]
This way	**Tudy** [tudɪ]

Turn right.	**Odbočte doprava.** [odbotʃtɛ doprava]
Turn left.	**Odbočte doleva.** [odbotʃtɛ dolɛva]
first (second, third) turn	**první (druhá, třetí) odbočka** [prvni: (druha:, trʒɛti:) odbotʃka]
to the right	**doprava** [doprava]

to the left

doleva
[dolɛva]

Go straight ahead.

Jděte stále rovně.
[jdetɛ staːlɛ rovne]

Signs

WELCOME!	VÍTEJTE! [vi:tɛjtɛ!]
ENTRANCE	VCHOD [vxot]
EXIT	VÝCHOD [vi:xot]

PUSH	TLAČIT [tlatʃɪt]
PULL	TÁHNOUT [ta:hnout]
OPEN	OTEVŘENO [otɛvrʒɛno]
CLOSED	ZAVŘENO [zavrʒɛno]

FOR WOMEN	ŽENY [ʒɛnɪ]
FOR MEN	MUŽI [muʒɪ]
GENTLEMEN, GENTS	PÁNI [pa:nɪ]
WOMEN	DÁMY [da:mɪ]

DISCOUNTS	VÝPRODEJ [vi:prodɛj]
SALE	VÝPRODEJ [vi:prodɛj]
FREE	ZDARMA [zdarma]
NEW!	NOVINKA! [novɪŋka!]
ATTENTION!	POZOR! [pozor!]

NO VACANCIES	PLNĚ OBSAZENO [plne opsazɛno]
RESERVED	REZERVACE [rɛzɛrvatsɛ]
ADMINISTRATION	VEDENÍ [vɛdɛni:]
STAFF ONLY	VSTUP JEN PRO ZAMĚSTNANCE [vstup jɛn pro zamnestnantsɛ]

BEWARE OF THE DOG!	**POZOR PES!** [pozor pɛs!]
NO SMOKING!	**ZÁKAZ KOUŘENÍ** [zaːkaz kourʒɛniː]
DO NOT TOUCH!	**NEDOTÝKEJTE SE** [nɛdotiːkɛjtɛ sɛ]
DANGEROUS	**ŽIVOTU NEBEZPEČNÉ** [ʒɪvotu nɛbɛzpɛtʃnɛː]
DANGER	**NEBEZPEČNÉ** [nɛbɛspɛtʃnɛː]
HIGH VOLTAGE	**VYSOKÉ NAPĚTÍ** [vɪsokɛː napetiː]
NO SWIMMING!	**ZÁKAZ KOUPÁNÍ** [zaːkaz koupaːniː]
OUT OF ORDER	**MIMO PROVOZ** [mɪmo provos]
FLAMMABLE	**HOŘLAVÉ** [horʒlavɛː]
FORBIDDEN	**ZAKÁZÁNO** [zakaːzaːno]
NO TRESPASSING!	**ZÁKAZ VSTUPU** [zaːkaz vstupu]
WET PAINT	**ČERSTVĚ NATŘENO** [tʃerstve natrʃeno]
CLOSED FOR RENOVATIONS	**UZAVŘENO Z DŮVODU REKONSTRUKCE** [uzavrʒeno z duːvodu rɛkonstruktsɛ]
WORKS AHEAD	**PRÁCE NA SILNICI** [praːtsɛ na sɪlnɪtsɪ]
DETOUR	**OBJÍŽĎKA** [objiːʒdᵗka]

Transportation. General phrases

plane	**letadlo** [lɛtadlo]
train	**vlak** [vlak]
bus	**autobus** [autobus]
ferry	**trajekt** [trajɛkt]
taxi	**taxík** [taksi:k]
car	**auto** [auto]
schedule	**jízdní řád** [ji:zdni: rʒa:t]
Where can I see the schedule?	**Kde se můžu podívat na jízdní řád?** [gdɛ sɛ mu:ʒu podi:vat na ji:zdni: rʒa:t?]
workdays (weekdays)	**pracovní dny** [pratsovni: dnɪ]
weekends	**víkendy** [vi:kɛndɪ]
holidays	**prázdniny** [pra:zdnɪnɪ]
DEPARTURE	**ODJEZD** [odjɛst]
ARRIVAL	**PŘÍJEZD** [prʃi:jɛst]
DELAYED	**ZPOŽDĚNÍ** [zpoʒdeni:]
CANCELLED	**ZRUŠENO** [zruʃɛno]
next (train, etc.)	**příští** [prʃi:ʃti:]
first	**první** [prvni:]
last	**poslední** [poslɛdni:]
When is the next ...?	**Kdy jede příští ...?** [gdɪ jɛdɛ prʒi:ʃti: ...?]
When is the first ...?	**Kdy jede první ...?** [gdɪ jɛdɛ prvni: ...?]

When is the last ...?

Kdy jede poslední ...?
[gdɪ jɛdɛ poslɛdni: ...?]

transfer (change of trains, etc.)

přestup
[prʃɛstup]

to make a transfer

přestoupit
[prʃɛstoupɪt]

Do I need to make a transfer?

Musím přestupovat?
[musi:m prʃɛstupovat?]

Buying tickets

Where can I buy tickets?	**Kde si mohu koupit jízdenky?** [gdɛ sɪ mohu koupɪt ji:zdɛŋkɪ?]
ticket	**jízdenka** [ji:zdɛŋka]
to buy a ticket	**koupit si jízdenku** [koupɪt sɪ ji:zdɛŋku]
ticket price	**cena jízdenky** [tsɛna ji:zdɛŋkɪ]
Where to?	**Kam?** [kam?]
To what station?	**Do jaké stanice?** [do jakɛ: stanɪtsɛ?]
I need ...	**Potřebuju ...** [potrʒɛbuju ...]
one ticket	**jednu jízdenku** [jɛdnu ji:zdɛŋku]
two tickets	**dvě jízdenky** [dve ji:zdɛŋkɪ]
three tickets	**tři jízdenky** [trʒɪ ji:zdɛŋkɪ]
one-way	**jízdenka jedním směrem** [ji:zdɛŋka jɛdni:m smnerɛm]
round-trip	**zpáteční jízdenka** [zpa:tɛtʃni: ji:zdɛŋka]
first class	**první třída** [prvni: trʒi:da]
second class	**druhá třída** [druha: trʒi:da]
today	**dnes** [dnɛs]
tomorrow	**zítra** [zi:tra]
the day after tomorrow	**pozítří** [pozi:trʃi:]
in the morning	**dopoledne** [dopolɛdnɛ]
in the afternoon	**odpoledne** [otpolɛdnɛ]
in the evening	**večer** [vɛtʃɛr]

aisle seat	**sedadlo u uličky** [sɛdadlo u ulɪtʃkɪ]
window seat	**sedadlo u okna** [sɛdadlo u okna]
How much?	**Kolik?** [kolɪk?]
Can I pay by credit card?	**Můžu platit kreditní kartou?** [muːʒu platɪt krɛdɪtniː kartou?]

Bus

bus	**autobus** [autobus]
intercity bus	**meziměstský autobus** [mɛzɪmnestski: autobus]
bus stop	**autobusová zastávka** [autobusova: zasta:fka]
Where's the nearest bus stop?	**Kde je nejbližší autobusová zastávka?** [gdɛ jɛ nɛjblɪʒʃi: autobusova: zasta:fka?]

number (bus ~, etc.)	**číslo** [tʃi:slo]
Which bus do I take to get to ...?	**Jakým autobusem se dostanu do ...?** [jaki:m autobusɛm sɛ dostanu do ...?]
Does this bus go to ...?	**Jede tento autobus do ...?** [jɛdɛ tɛnto autobus do ...?]
How frequent are the buses?	**Jak často jezdí tento autobus?** [jak tʃasto jɛzdi: tɛnto autobus?]

every 15 minutes	**každých patnáct minut** [kaʒdi:x patna:tst mɪnut]
every half hour	**každou půlhodinu** [kaʒdou pu:lhodɪnu]
every hour	**každou hodinu** [kaʒdou hodɪnu]
several times a day	**několikrát za den** [nekolɪkra:t za dɛn]
... times a day	**... krát za den** [... kra:t za dɛn]

schedule	**jízdní řád** [ji:zdni: rʒa:t]
Where can I see the schedule?	**Kde se můžu podívat na jízdní řád?** [gdɛ sɛ mu:ʒu podi:vat na ji:zdni: rʒa:t?]
When is the next bus?	**Kdy jede příští autobus?** [gdɪ jɛdɛ prʒi:ʃti: autobus?]
When is the first bus?	**Kdy jede první autobus?** [gdɪ jɛdɛ prvni: autobus?]
When is the last bus?	**Kdy jede poslední autobus?** [gdɪ jɛdɛ poslɛdni: autobus?]

stop	**zastávka** [zasta:fka]
next stop	**příští zastávka** [prʃi:ʃti: zasta:fka]

last stop (terminus)

poslední zastávka
[poslɛdni: zasta:fka]

Stop here, please.

Zastavte tady, prosím.
[zastaftɛ tadɪ, prosi:m]

Excuse me, this is my stop.

Promiňte, já tady vystupuju.
[promɪnʲtɛ, ja: tadɪ vɪstupuju]

Train

train	**vlak** [vlak]
suburban train	**příměstský vlak** [prʒi:mnestskɪ vlak]
long-distance train	**dálkový vlak** [da:lkovi: vlak]
train station	**vlakové nádraží** [vlakovɛ: na:draʒi:]
Excuse me, where is the exit to the platform?	**Promiňte, kde je vstup na nástupiště?** [promɪnʲtɛ, gdɛ jɛ vstup na na:stupɪʃtɛ?]
Does this train go to ...?	**Jede tento vlak do ...?** [jɛdɛ tɛnto vlak do ...?]
next train	**příští vlak** [prʃi:ʃti: vlak]
When is the next train?	**Kdy jede příští vlak?** [gdɪ jɛdɛ prʒi:ʃti: vlak?]
Where can I see the schedule?	**Kde se můžu podívat na jízdní řád?** [gdɛ sɛ mu:ʒu podi:vat na ji:zdni: rʒa:t?]
From which platform?	**Ze kterého nástupiště?** [zɛ ktɛrɛ:ho na:stupɪʃtɛ?]
When does the train arrive in ...?	**Kdy přijede tento vlak do ...?** [gdɪ prʃɪjɛdɛ tɛnto vlak do ...?]
Please help me.	**Můžete mi prosím pomoct?** [mu:ʒetɛ mɪ prosi:m pomotst?]
I'm looking for my seat.	**Hledám své místo.** [hlɛda:m svɛ: mi:sto]
We're looking for our seats.	**Hledáme svá místa.** [hlɛda:mɛ sva: mi:sta]
My seat is taken.	**Moje místo je obsazeno.** [mojɛ mi:sto jɛ opsazɛno]
Our seats are taken.	**Naše místa jsou obsazena.** [naʃɛ mi:sta jsou opsazɛna]
I'm sorry but this is my seat.	**Promiňte, ale toto je moje místo.** [promɪnʲtɛ, alɛ toto jɛ mojɛ mi:sto]
Is this seat taken?	**Je toto místo volné?** [jɛ toto mi:sto volnɛ:?]
May I sit here?	**Můžu si zde sednout?** [mu:ʒu sɪ zdɛ sɛdnout?]

On the train. Dialogue (No ticket)

Ticket, please.

I don't have a ticket.

I lost my ticket.

I forgot my ticket at home.

Jízdenku, prosím.
[ji:zdɛŋku, prosi:m]

Nemám jízdenku.
[nɛma:m ji:zdɛŋku]

Ztratil jsem jízdenku.
[stratɪl jsɛm ji:zdɛŋku]

Zapomněl svou jízdenku doma.
[zapomel svou ji:zdɛŋku doma]

You can buy a ticket from me.

You will also have to pay a fine.

Okay.

Where are you going?

I'm going to …

Jízdenku si můžete koupit u mě.
[ji:zdɛŋku sɪ mu:ʒetɛ koupɪt u mne]

Také budete muset zaplatit pokutu.
[takɛ: budɛtɛ musɛt zaplatɪt pokutu]

Dobrá.
[dobra:]

Kam jedete?
[kam jɛdɛtɛ?]

Jedu do …
[jɛdu do …]

How much? I don't understand.

Write it down, please.

Okay. Can I pay with a credit card?

Yes, you can.

Kolik? Nerozumím.
[kolɪk? nɛrozumi:m]

Napište to, prosím.
[napɪʃtɛ to, prosi:m]

Dobrá. Můžu platit kreditní kartou?
[dobra:. mu:ʒu platɪt krɛdɪtni: kartou?]

Ano, můžete.
[ano, mu:ʒetɛ]

Here's your receipt.

Sorry about the fine.

That's okay. It was my fault.

Enjoy your trip.

Tady je vaše stvrzenka.
[tadɪ jɛ vaʃɛ stvrzɛŋka]

Omlouvám se za tu pokutu.
[omlouva:m sɛ za tu pokutu]

To je v pořádku. Je to moje chyba.
[to jɛ v porʒa:tku. jɛ to mojɛ xɪba]

Příjemnou cestu.
[prʒi:jɛmnou tsɛstu]

Taxi

taxi	**taxík** [taksi:k]
taxi driver	**taxikář** [taksɪka:rʒ]
to catch a taxi	**chytit si taxík** [xɪtɪt sɪ taksi:k]
taxi stand	**stanoviště taxíků** [stanovɪʃte taksi:ku:]
Where can I get a taxi?	**Kde můžu sehnat taxík?** [gdɛ mu:ʒu sɛhnat taksi:k?]

to call a taxi	**volat taxík** [volat taksi:k]
I need a taxi.	**Potřebuju taxík.** [potrʒɛbuju taksi:k]
Right now.	**Hned teď.** [hnɛt tɛtʲ]
What is your address (location)?	**Jaká je vaše adresa?** [jaka: jɛ vaʃɛ adrɛsa?]
My address is …	**Moje adresa je …** [mojɛ adrɛsa jɛ …]
Your destination?	**Váš cíl?** [va:ʃ tsi:l?]
Excuse me, …	**Promiňte, …** [promɪnʲtɛ, …]
Are you available?	**Jste volný?** [jstɛ volni:?]
How much is it to get to …?	**Kolik to stojí do …?** [kolɪk to stoji: do …?]
Do you know where it is?	**Víte, kde to je?** [vi:tɛ, gdɛ to jɛ?]

Airport, please.	**Na letiště, prosím.** [na lɛtɪʃte, prosi:m]
Stop here, please.	**Zastavte tady, prosím.** [zastaftɛ tadɪ, prosi:m]
It's not here.	**To není tady.** [to nɛni: tadɪ]
This is the wrong address.	**To je nesprávná adresa.** [to jɛ nɛspra:vna: adrɛsa]
Turn left.	**Zabočte doleva.** [zabotʃtɛ dolɛva]
Turn right.	**Zabočte doprava.** [zabotʃtɛ doprava]

How much do I owe you?

Kolik vám dlužím?
[kolɪk va:m dluʒi:m?]

I'd like a receipt, please.

Chtěl /Chtěla/ bych stvrzenku, prosím.
[xtel /xtela/ bɪx stvrzɛŋku, prosi:m]

Keep the change.

Drobné si nechte.
[drobnɛ: sɪ nɛxtɛ]

Would you please wait for me?

Můžete tady na mě počkat?
[mu:ʒetɛ tadɪ na mne potʃkat?]

five minutes

pět minut
[pet mɪnut]

ten minutes

deset minut
[dɛsɛt mɪnut]

fifteen minutes

patnáct minut
[patna:tst mɪnut]

twenty minutes

dvacet minut
[dvatsɛt mɪnut]

half an hour

půl hodiny
[pu:l hodɪnɪ]

Hotel

Hello.

Dobrý den.
[dobrɪ: dɛn]

My name is …

Jmenuju se …
[jmɛnuju sɛ …]

I have a reservation.

Mám tady rezervaci.
[ma:m tadɪ rɛzɛrvatsɪ]

I need …

Potřebuju …
[potrʒɛbuju …]

a single room

jednolůžkový pokoj
[jɛdnolu:ʃkovi: pokoj]

a double room

dvoulůžkový pokoj
[dvoulu:ʃkovi: pokoj]

How much is that?

Kolik to stojí?
[kolɪk to stoji:?]

That's a bit expensive.

To je trochu drahé.
[to jɛ troxu drahɛ:]

Do you have anything else?

Máte nějaké další možnosti?
[ma:tɛ nejakɛ: dalʃi: moʒnostɪ?]

I'll take it.

To si vezmu.
[to sɪ vɛzmu]

I'll pay in cash.

Budu platit v hotovosti.
[budu platɪt v hotovostɪ]

I've got a problem.

Mám problém.
[ma:m problɛ:m]

My … is broken.

… je rozbitý /rozbitá/.
[… jɛ rozbɪtɪ: /rozbɪta:/]

My … is out of order.

… je mimo provoz.
[… jɛ mɪmo provoz]

TV

Můj televizor …
[mu:j tɛlɛvɪzor …]

air conditioner

Moje klimatizace …
[mojɛ klɪmatɪzatsɛ …]

tap

Můj kohoutek …
[mu:j kohoutɛk …]

shower

Moje sprcha …
[mojɛ sprxa …]

sink

Můj dřez …
[mu:j drʒɛz …]

safe

Můj sejf …
[mu:j sɛjf …]

door lock	**Můj zámek ...** [mu:j za:mɛk ...]
electrical outlet	**Moje elektrická zásuvka ...** [mojɛ ɛlɛktrɪtska: za:sufka ...]
hairdryer	**Můj fén ...** [mu:j fɛ:n ...]

I don't have ...	**Nemám ...** [nɛma:m ...]
water	**vodu** [vodu]
light	**světlo** [svetlo]
electricity	**elektřinu** [ɛlɛktrʒɪnu]

Can you give me ...?	**Můžete mi dát ...?** [mu:ʒetɛ mɪ da:t ...?]
a towel	**ručník** [rutʃni:k]
a blanket	**přikrývku** [prʒɪkri:fku]
slippers	**bačkory** [batʃkorɪ]
a robe	**župan** [ʒupan]
shampoo	**šampón** [ʃampón]
soap	**mýdlo** [mi:dlo]

I'd like to change rooms.	**Chtěl bych vyměnit pokoje.** [xtel bɪx vɪmnenɪt pokojɛ]
I can't find my key.	**Nemůžu najít klíč.** [nɛmu:ʒu naji:t kli:tʃ]
Could you open my room, please?	**Můžete mi otevřít pokoj, prosím?** [mu:ʒetɛ mɪ otɛvrʒi:t pokoj, prosi:m?]
Who's there?	**Kdo je tam?** [gdo jɛ tam?]
Come in!	**Vstupte!** [vstuptɛ!]
Just a minute!	**Minutku!** [mɪnutku!]
Not right now, please.	**Teď ne, prosím.** [tɛtʲ nɛ, prosi:m]

Come to my room, please.	**Pojďte do mého pokoje, prosím.** [pojdʲtɛ do mɛ:ho pokojɛ, prosi:m]
I'd like to order food service.	**Chtěl bych si objednat jídlo.** [xtel bɪx sɪ objɛdnat ji:dlo]
My room number is ...	**Číslo mého pokoje je ...** [tʃi:slo mɛ:ho pokojɛ jɛ ...]

I'm leaving ...	**Odjíždím ...** [odji:ʒdi:m ...]
We're leaving ...	**Odjíždíme ...** [odji:ʒdi:mɛ ...]
right now	**hned teď** [hnɛt tɛtʲ]
this afternoon	**dnes odpoledne** [dnɛs otpolɛdnɛ]
tonight	**dnes večer** [dnɛs vɛtʃɛr]
tomorrow	**zítra** [zi:tra]
tomorrow morning	**zítra dopoledne** [zi:tra dopolɛdnɛ]
tomorrow evening	**zítra večer** [zi:tra vɛtʃɛr]
the day after tomorrow	**pozítří** [pozi:trʃi:]

I'd like to pay.	**Chtěl bych zaplatit.** [xtel bɪx zaplatɪt]
Everything was wonderful.	**Všechno bylo skvělé.** [vʃɛxno bɪlo skvelɛ:]
Where can I get a taxi?	**Kde můžu sehnat taxík?** [gdɛ mu:ʒu sɛhnat taksi:k?]
Would you call a taxi for me, please?	**Můžete mi zavolat taxík, prosím?** [mu:ʒetɛ mɪ zavolat taksi:k, prosi:m?]

Restaurant

Can I look at the menu, please?	**Můžu se podívat na jídelní lístek, prosím?** [muːʒu sɛ podiːvat na jiːdɛlniː liːstɛk, prosiːm?]
Table for one.	**Stůl pro jednoho.** [stuːl pro jɛdnoho]
There are two (three, four) of us.	**Jsme dva (tři, čtyři).** [jsmɛ dva (tr̝ɪ, tʃtɪr̝ɪ)]

Smoking	**Kuřáci** [kur̝aːtsɪ]
No smoking	**Nekuřáci** [nɛkur̝aːtsɪ]
Excuse me! (addressing a waiter)	**Promiňte!** [promɪɲtɛ!]
menu	**jídelní lístek** [jiːdɛlniː liːstɛk]
wine list	**vinný lístek** [vɪnnɪ liːstɛk]
The menu, please.	**Jídelní lístek, prosím.** [jiːdɛlniː liːstɛk, prosiːm]
Are you ready to order?	**Vybrali jste si?** [vɪbralɪ jstɛ sɪ?]
What will you have?	**Co si dáte?** [tso sɪ daːtɛ?]
I'll have …	**Dám si …** [daːm sɪ …]

I'm a vegetarian.	**Jsem vegetarián.** [jsɛm vɛgɛtaria:n]
meat	**maso** [maso]
fish	**ryba** [r̝ɪba]
vegetables	**zelenina** [zɛlɛnɪna]
Do you have vegetarian dishes?	**Máte vegetariánská jídla?** [maːtɛ vɛgɛtaria:nska: jiːdla?]
I don't eat pork.	**Nejím vepřové.** [nɛjiːm vɛpr̝ovɛː]
Band-Aid	**On /ona/ nejí maso.** [on /ona/ nɛjiː maso]
I am allergic to …	**Jsem alergický /alergická/ na …** [jsɛm alɛrgɪtski: /alɛrgɪtska:/ na …]

Would you please bring me ... | **Přinesl byste mi prosím ...**
[prʒɪnɛsl bɪstɛ mɪ prosi:m ...]

salt | pepper | sugar | **sůl | pepř | cukr**
[su:l | pɛprʒ | tsukr]

coffee | tea | dessert | **kávu | čaj | zákusek**
[ka:vu | tʃaj | za:kusɛk]

water | sparkling | plain | **vodu | perlivou | neperlivou**
[vodu | pɛrlɪvou | nɛpɛrlɪvou]

a spoon | fork | knife | **lžíci | vidličku | nůž**
[lʒi:tsɪ | vɪdlɪtʃku | nu:ʒ]

a plate | napkin | **talíř | ubrousek**
[tali:rʒ | ubrousɛk]

Enjoy your meal! | **Dobrou chuť!**
[dobrou xutʲ!]

One more, please. | **Ještě jednou, prosím.**
[jɛʃte jɛdnou, prosi:m]

It was very delicious. | **Bylo to výborné.**
[bɪlo to vi:bornɛ:]

---

check | change | tip | **účet | drobné | spropitné**
[u:tʃɛt | drobnɛ: | spropɪtnɛ:]

Check, please.
(Could I have the check, please?) | **Účet, prosím.**
[u:tʃɛt, prosi:m]

Can I pay by credit card? | **Můžu platit kreditní kartou?**
[mu:ʒu platɪt krɛdɪtni: kartou?]

I'm sorry, there's a mistake here. | **Omlouvám se, ale tady je chyba.**
[omlouva:m sɛ, alɛ tadɪ jɛ xɪba]

Shopping

Can I help you?

Co si přejete?
[tso sɪ prʒɛjɛtɛ?]

Do you have ...?

Máte ...?
[maːtɛ ...?]

I'm looking for ...

Hledám ...
[hlɛdaːm ...]

I need ...

Potřebuju ...
[potrʒɛbuju ...]

I'm just looking.

Jen se dívám.
[jɛn sɛ diːvaːm]

We're just looking.

Jen se díváme.
[jɛn sɛ diːvaːmɛ]

I'll come back later.

Vrátím se později.
[vraːtiːm sɛ pozdejɪ]

We'll come back later.

Vrátíme se později.
[vraːtiːmɛ sɛ pozdejɪ]

discounts | sale

slevy | výprodej
[slɛvɪ | viːprodɛj]

Would you please show me ...

Můžete mi prosím ukázat ...
[muːʒetɛ mɪ prosiːm ukaːzat ...]

Would you please give me ...

Můžete mi prosím dát ...
[muːʒetɛ mɪ prosiːm daːt ...]

Can I try it on?

Můžu si to vyzkoušet?
[muːʒu sɪ to vɪskouʃɛt?]

Excuse me, where's the fitting room?

Promiňte, kde je zkušební kabinka?
[promɪnʲtɛ, gdɛ jɛ skuʃɛbniː kabɪŋka?]

Which color would you like?

Jakou byste chtěl /chtěla/ barvu?
[jakou bɪstɛ xtel /xtela/ barvu?]

size | length

velikost | délku
[vɛlɪkost | dɛːlku]

How does it fit?

Jak vám to sedí?
[jak vaːm to sɛdiː?]

How much is it?

Kolik to stojí?
[kolɪk to stojiː?]

That's too expensive.

To je příliš drahé.
[to jɛ prʃiːlɪʃ drahɛː]

I'll take it.

Vezmu si to.
[vɛzmu sɪ to]

Excuse me, where do I pay?

Promiňte, kde můžu zaplatit?
[promɪnʲtɛ, gdɛ muːʒu zaplatɪt?]

Will you pay in cash or credit card?

Budete platit v hotovosti nebo kreditní kartou?
[budɛtɛ platɪt v hotovostɪ nɛbo krɛdɪtni: kartou?]

In cash | with credit card

v hotovosti | kreditní kartou
[v hotovostɪ | krɛdɪtni: kartou]

Do you want the receipt?

Chcete stvrzenku?
[xtsɛtɛ stvrzɛŋku?]

Yes, please.

Ano, prosím.
[ano, prosi:m]

No, it's OK.

Ne, to je dobré.
[nɛ, to jɛ dobrɛ:]

Thank you. Have a nice day!

Děkuji. Hezký den.
[dekujɪ. hɛski: dɛn]

In town

Excuse me, ...	**Promiňte, prosím.** [promɪnˈtɛ, prosiːm]
I'm looking for ...	**Hledám ...** [hlɛdaːm ...]
the subway	**metro** [mɛtro]
my hotel	**svůj hotel** [svuːj hotɛl]
the movie theater	**kino** [kɪno]
a taxi stand	**stanoviště taxíků** [stanovɪʃte taksiːkuː]

an ATM	**bankomat** [baŋkomat]
a foreign exchange office	**směnárnu** [smnenaːrnu]
an internet café	**internetovou kavárnu** [ɪntɛrnɛtovou kavaːrnu]
... street	**... ulici** [... ulɪtsɪ]
this place	**toto místo** [toto miːsto]

Do you know where ... is?	**Nevíte, kde je ...?** [nɛviːtɛ, gdɛ jɛ ...?]
Which street is this?	**Jaká je toto ulice?** [jakaː jɛ toto ulɪtsɛ?]
Show me where we are right now.	**Ukažte mi, kde teď jsme.** [ukaʃtɛ mɪ, gdɛ tɛdʲ jsmɛ]
Can I get there on foot?	**Dostanu se tam pěšky?** [dostanu sɛ tam pɛʃkɪ?]
Do you have a map of the city?	**Máte mapu tohoto města?** [maːtɛ mapu tohoto mnesta?]

How much is a ticket to get in?	**Kolik stojí vstupenka?** [kolɪk stojiː vstupɛŋka?]
Can I take pictures here?	**Můžu tady fotit?** [muːʒu tadɪ fotɪt?]
Are you open?	**Máte otevřeno?** [maːtɛ otɛvrʒɛno?]

When do you open?

Kdy otvíráte?
[gdɪ otviːraːtɛ?]

When do you close?

Kdy zavíráte?
[gdɪ zaviːraːtɛ?]

Money

money	**peníze**
	[pɛniːzɛ]
cash	**hotovost**
	[hotovost]
paper money	**papírové peníze**
	[papiːrovɛː pɛniːzɛ]
loose change	**drobné**
	[drobnɛː]
check | change | tip	**účet | drobné | spropitné**
	[uːtʃɛt | drobnɛː | spropɪtnɛː]

credit card	**kreditní karta**
	[krɛdɪtni: karta]
wallet	**peněženka**
	[pɛnɛʒɛŋka]
to buy	**koupit**
	[koupɪt]
to pay	**platit**
	[platɪt]
fine	**pokuta**
	[pokuta]
free	**zdarma**
	[zdarma]

Where can I buy ...?	**Kde dostanu koupit ...?**
	[gdɛ dostanu koupɪt ...?]
Is the bank open now?	**Je teď otevřená banka?**
	[jɛ tɛdʲ otɛvrʒɛna: baŋka?]
When does it open?	**Kdy otvírají?**
	[gdɪ otviːraji:?]
When does it close?	**Kdy zavírají?**
	[gdɪ zaviːraji:?]

How much?	**Kolik?**
	[kolɪk?]
How much is this?	**Kolik to stojí?**
	[kolɪk to stoji:?]
That's too expensive.	**To je příliš drahé.**
	[to jɛ prʃiːlɪʃ drahɛː]

Excuse me, where do I pay?	**Promiňte, kde můžu zaplatit?**
	[promɪnʲtɛ, gdɛ muːʒu zaplatɪt?]
Check, please.	**Účet, prosím.**
	[uːtʃɛt, prosiːm]

Can I pay by credit card?

Is there an ATM here?

I'm looking for an ATM.

Můžu platit kreditní kartou?
[mu:ʒu platɪt krɛdɪtni: kartou?]
Je tady bankomat?
[jɛ tadɪ baŋkomat?]
Hledám bankomat.
[hlɛda:m baŋkomat]

I'm looking for a foreign exchange office.

I'd like to change …

What is the exchange rate?

Do you need my passport?

Hledám směnárnu.
[hlɛda:m smnena:rnu]
Chtěl bych si vyměnit …
[xtel bɪx sɪ vɪmnenɪt …]
Jaký je kurz?
[jaki: jɛ kurs?]
Potřebujete můj pas?
[potrʒɛbujɛtɛ mu:j pas?]

Time

What time is it?	**Kolik je hodin?** [kolɪk jɛ hodɪn?]
When?	**Kdy?** [gdɪ?]
At what time?	**V kolik hodin?** [v kolɪk hodɪn?]
now | later | after …	**teď | později | po …** [tɛdʲ | pozdejɪ | po …]
one o'clock	**jedna hodina** [jɛdna hodɪna]
one fifteen	**čtvrt na dvě** [tʃtvrt na dve]
one thirty	**půl druhé** [puːl druhɛː]
one forty-five	**tři čtvrtě na dvě** [trʒɪ tʃtvrte na dve]
one | two | three	**jedna | dvě | tři** [jɛdna | dve | trʒɪ]
four | five | six	**čtyři | pět | šest** [tʃtɪrʒɪ | pet | ʃɛst]
seven | eight | nine	**sedm | osm | devět** [sɛdm | osm | dɛvet]
ten | eleven | twelve	**deset | jedenáct | dvanáct** [dɛsɛt | jɛdɛnaːtst | dvanaːtst]
in …	**za …** [za …]
five minutes	**pět minut** [pet mɪnut]
ten minutes	**deset minut** [dɛsɛt mɪnut]
fifteen minutes	**patnáct minut** [patnaːtst mɪnut]
twenty minutes	**dvacet minut** [dvatsɛt mɪnut]
half an hour	**půl hodiny** [puːl hodɪnɪ]
an hour	**hodinu** [hodɪnu]

in the morning	dopoledne [dopolɛdnɛ]
early in the morning	brzy ráno [brzɪ ra:no]
this morning	dnes dopoledne [dnɛs dopolɛdnɛ]
tomorrow morning	zítra dopoledne [zi:tra dopolɛdnɛ]

in the middle of the day	v poledne [v polɛdnɛ]
in the afternoon	odpoledne [otpolɛdnɛ]
in the evening	večer [vɛtʃɛr]
tonight	dnes večer [dnɛs vɛtʃɛr]

at night	v noci [v notsɪ]
yesterday	včera [vtʃɛra]
today	dnes [dnɛs]
tomorrow	zítra [zi:tra]
the day after tomorrow	pozítří [pozi:trʃi:]

What day is it today?	Kolikátého je dnes? [kolɪka:tɛ:ho jɛ dnɛs?]
It's ...	Dnes je ... [dnɛs jɛ ...]
Monday	pondělí [pondeli:]
Tuesday	úterý [u:tɛri:]
Wednesday	středa [strʒɛda]

Thursday	čtvrtek [tʃtvrtɛk]
Friday	pátek [pa:tɛk]
Saturday	sobota [sobota]
Sunday	neděle [nɛdelɛ]

Greetings. Introductions

Hello.	**Dobrý den.** [dobri: dɛn]
Pleased to meet you.	**Těší mě, že vás poznávám.** [teʃi: mne, ʒe va:s pozna:va:m]
Me too.	**Mě také.** [mne takɛ:]
I'd like you to meet …	**Rád /Ráda/ bych** **vás seznámil /seznámila/ …** [ra:d /ra:da/ bɪx va:s sɛzna:mɪl /sɛzna:mɪla/ …]
Nice to meet you.	**Těší mě.** [teʃi: mne]

How are you?	**Jak se máte?** [jak sɛ ma:tɛ?]
My name is …	**Jmenuju se …** [jmɛnuju sɛ …]
His name is …	**On se jmenuje …** [on sɛ jmɛnujɛ …]
Her name is …	**Ona se jmenuje …** [ona sɛ jmɛnujɛ …]
What's your name?	**Jak se jmenujete?** [jak sɛ jmɛnujɛtɛ?]
What's his name?	**Jak se jmenuje?** [jak sɛ jmɛnujɛ?]
What's her name?	**Jak se jmenuje?** [jak sɛ jmɛnujɛ?]

What's your last name?	**Jaké je vaše příjmení?** [jakɛ: jɛ vaʃɛ prʒi:jmɛni:?]
You can call me …	**Můžete mi říkat …** [mu:ʒɛtɛ mɪ rʒi:kat …]
Where are you from?	**Odkud jste?** [otkut jstɛ?]
I'm from …	**Jsem z …** [jsɛm s …]
What do you do for a living?	**Čím jste?** [tʃi:m jstɛ?]

Who is this?	**Kdo to je?** [gdo to jɛ?]
Who is he?	**Kdo je on?** [gdo jɛ on?]

Who is she?	**Kdo je ona?** [gdo jɛ ona?]
Who are they?	**Kdo jsou oni?** [gdo jsou onɪ?]

This is ...	**To je ...** [to jɛ ...]
my friend (masc.)	**můj přítel** [muːj prʃiːtɛl]
my friend (fem.)	**moje přítelkyně** [mojɛ prʃiːtɛlkɪne]
my husband	**můj manžel** [muːj manʒel]
my wife	**moje manželka** [mojɛ manʒelka]

my father	**můj otec** [muːj otɛts]
my mother	**moje matka** [mojɛ matka]
my brother	**můj bratr** [muːj bratr]
my sister	**moje sestra** [mojɛ sɛstra]
my son	**můj syn** [muːj sɪn]
my daughter	**moje dcera** [mojɛ dtsɛra]

This is our son.	**To je náš syn.** [to jɛ naːʃ sɪn]
This is our daughter.	**To je naše dcera.** [to jɛ naʃɛ dtsɛra]
These are my children.	**To jsou moje děti.** [to jsou mojɛ detɪ]
These are our children.	**To jsou naše děti.** [to jsou naʃɛ detɪ]

Farewells

Good bye!	**Na shledanou!** [na sxlɛdanou!]
Bye! (inform.)	**Ahoj!** [ahoj!]
See you tomorrow.	**Uvidíme se zítra.** [uvɪdi:mɛ sɛ zi:tra]
See you soon.	**Brzy ahoj.** [brzɪ ahoj]
See you at seven.	**Ahoj v sedm.** [ahoj v sɛdm]
Have fun!	**Hezkou zábavu!** [hɛskou za:bavu!]
Talk to you later.	**Promluvíme si později.** [promluvi:mɛ sɪ pozdejɪ]
Have a nice weekend.	**Hezký víkend.** [hɛskɪ vi:kɛnt]
Good night.	**Dobrou noc.** [dobrou nots]
It's time for me to go.	**Už musím jít.** [uʒ musi:m ji:t]
I have to go.	**Musím jít.** [musi:m ji:t]
I will be right back.	**Hned se vrátím.** [hnɛt sɛ vra:ti:m]
It's late.	**Je pozdě.** [jɛ pozde]
I have to get up early.	**Musím brzy vstávat.** [musi:m brzɪ vsta:vat]
I'm leaving tomorrow.	**Zítra odjíždím.** [zi:tra odji:ʒdi:m]
We're leaving tomorrow.	**Zítra odjíždíme.** [zi:tra odji:ʒdi:mɛ]
Have a nice trip!	**Hezký výlet!** [hɛski: vɪlɛt!]
It was nice meeting you.	**Jsem rád /ráda/,** **že jsem vás poznal /poznala/.** [jsɛm ra:d /ra:da/, ʒe jsɛm va:s poznal /poznala/]

It was nice talking to you.	**Rád /Ráda/ jsem si s vámi popovídal /popovídala/.** [ra:d /ra:da/ jsɛm sɪ s va:mɪ popovi:dal /popovi:dala/]
Thanks for everything.	**Děkuji vám za všechno.** [dekujɪ va:m za vʃɛxno]

I had a very good time.	**Měl /Měla/ jsem se moc dobře.** [mnel /mnela/ jsɛm sɛ mots dobrʒɛ]
We had a very good time.	**Měli /Měly/ jsme se moc dobře.** [mnelɪ /mnelɪ/ jsmɛ sɛ mots dobrʒɛ]
It was really great.	**Bylo to fakt skvělé.** [bɪlo to fakt skvelɛ:]
I'm going to miss you.	**Bude se mi po tobě stýskat.** [budɛ sɛ mɪ po tobe sti:skat]
We're going to miss you.	**Bude se nám po vás stýskat.** [budɛ sɛ na:m po va:s sti:skat]

Good luck!	**Hodně štěstí!** [hodne ʃtesti:!]
Say hi to …	**Pozdravuj …** [pozdravuj …]

Foreign language

I don't understand.	**Nerozumím.** [nɛrozumi:m]
Write it down, please.	**Napište to, prosím.** [napɪʃtɛ to, prosi:m]
Do you speak ...?	**Mluvíte ...?** [mluvi:tɛ ...?]

I speak a little bit of ...	**Mluvím trochu ...** [mluvi:m troxu ...]
English	**anglicky** [anglɪtskɪ]
Turkish	**turecky** [turɛtskɪ]
Arabic	**arabsky** [arapskɪ]
French	**francouzsky** [frantsouskɪ]

German	**německy** [nemɛtskɪ]
Italian	**italsky** [ɪtalskɪ]
Spanish	**španělsky** [ʃpanelskɪ]
Portuguese	**portugalsky** [portugalskɪ]
Chinese	**čínsky** [tʃi:nskɪ]
Japanese	**japonsky** [japonskɪ]

Can you repeat that, please.	**Můžete to prosím zopakovat.** [mu:ʒetɛ to prosi:m zopakovat]
I understand.	**Rozumím.** [rozumi:m]
I don't understand.	**Nerozumím.** [nɛrozumi:m]
Please speak more slowly.	**Mluvte prosím pomalu.** [mluftɛ prosi:m pomalu]

Is that correct? (Am I saying it right?)	**Je to správně?** [jɛ to spra:vne?]
What is this? (What does this mean?)	**Co to je?** [tso to jɛ?]

Apologies

Excuse me, please.
Promiňte, prosím.
[promɪnˈtɛ, prosiːm]

I'm sorry.
Omlouvám se.
[omlouvaːm sɛ]

I'm really sorry.
Je mi to opravdu líto.
[jɛ mɪ to opravdu liːto]

Sorry, it's my fault.
Omlouvám se, je to moje chyba.
[omlouvaːm sɛ, jɛ to mojɛ xɪba]

My mistake.
Moje chyba.
[mojɛ xɪba]

May I ...?
Můžu ...?
[muːʒu ...?]

Do you mind if I ...?
Nevadilo by vám, kdybych ...?
[nɛvadɪlo bɪ vaːm, gdɪbɪx ...?]

It's OK.
Nic se nestalo.
[nɪts sɛ nɛstalo]

It's all right.
To je v pořádku.
[to jɛ v porʒaːtku]

Don't worry about it.
Tím se netrapte.
[tiːm sɛ nɛtraptɛ]

Agreement

Yes.	**Ano.** [ano]
Yes, sure.	**Ano, jistě.** [ano, jɪste]
OK (Good!)	**Dobrá.** [dobra:]
Very well.	**Dobře.** [dobrʒɛ]
Certainly!	**Samozřejmě!** [samozrʒɛjmne!]
I agree.	**Souhlasím.** [souhlasi:m]

That's correct.	**To je správně.** [to jɛ spra:vne]
That's right.	**To je v pořádku.** [to jɛ v porʒa:tku]
You're right.	**Máte pravdu.** [ma:tɛ pravdu]
I don't mind.	**Nevadí mi to.** [nɛvadi: mɪ to]
Absolutely right.	**To je naprosto správně.** [to jɛ naprosto spra:vne]

It's possible.	**Je to možné.** [jɛ to moʒnɛ:]
That's a good idea.	**To je dobrý nápad.** [to jɛ dobri: na:pat]
I can't say no.	**Nemůžu říct ne.** [nɛmu:ʒu rʒi:tst nɛ]
I'd be happy to.	**Hrozně rád /ráda/.** [hrozne ra:d /ra:da/]
With pleasure.	**S radostí.** [s radosti:]

Refusal. Expressing doubt

No.
Ne.
[nɛ]

Certainly not.
Určitě ne.
[urtʃɪte nɛ]

I don't agree.
Nesouhlasím.
[nɛsouhlasi:m]

I don't think so.
Myslím, že ne.
[mɪsli:m, ʒe nɛ]

It's not true.
To není pravda.
[to nɛni: pravda]

You are wrong.
Mýlíte se.
[mɪli:tɛ sɛ]

I think you are wrong.
Myslím, že se mýlíte.
[mɪsli:m, ʒe sɛ mí:li:tɛ]

I'm not sure.
Nejsem si jist /jista/.
[nɛjsɛm sɪ jɪst /jɪsta/]

It's impossible.
To je nemožné.
[to jɛ nɛmoʒnɛ:]

Nothing of the kind (sort)!
Nic takového!
[nɪts takovɛ:ho!]

The exact opposite.
Přesně naopak.
[prʃɛsne naopak]

I'm against it.
Jsem proti.
[jsɛm protɪ]

I don't care.
Je mi to jedno.
[jɛ mɪ to jɛdno]

I have no idea.
Nemám ani ponětí.
[nɛma:m anɪ poneti:]

I doubt it.
To pochybuju.
[to poxɪbuju]

Sorry, I can't.
Bohužel, nemůžu.
[bohuʒel, nɛmu:ʒu]

Sorry, I don't want to.
Bohužel, nechci.
[bohuʒel, nɛxtsɪ]

Thank you, but I don't need this.
Děkuju, ale to já nepotřebuju.
[dekuju, alɛ to ja: nɛpotrʒɛbuju]

It's getting late.
Už je pozdě.
[uʒ jɛ pozde]

I have to get up early.

Musím brzy vstávat.
[musi:m brzɪ vsta:vat]

I don't feel well.

Necítím se dobře.
[nɛtsi:ti:m sɛ dobrʒɛ]

Expressing gratitude

Thank you.	**Děkuju.** [dekuju]
Thank you very much.	**Děkuju mockrát.** [dekuju motskra:t]
I really appreciate it.	**Opravdu si toho vážím.** [opravdu sɪ toho va:ʒi:m]
I'm really grateful to you.	**Jsem vám opravdu vděčný /vděčná/.** [jsɛm va:m opravdu vdetʃni: /vdetʃna:/]
We are really grateful to you.	**Jsme vám opravdu vděční.** [jsmɛ va:m opravdu vdetʃni:]
Thank you for your time.	**Děkuju za váš čas.** [dekuju za va:ʃ tʃas]
Thanks for everything.	**Děkuju za všechno.** [dekuju za vʃɛxno]
Thank you for ...	**Děkuju za ...** [dekuju za ...]
your help	**vaši pomoc** [vaʃɪ pomots]
a nice time	**příjemně strávený čas** [prʒi:jemne stra:vɛnɪ tʃas]
a wonderful meal	**skvělé jídlo** [skvelɛ: ji:dlo]
a pleasant evening	**příjemný večer** [prʒi:jemnɪ vɛtʃɛr]
a wonderful day	**nádherný den** [na:dhɛrni: dɛn]
an amazing journey	**úžasnou cestu** [u:ʒasnou tsɛstu]
Don't mention it.	**To nestojí za řeč.** [to nɛstoji: za rʒɛtʃ]
You are welcome.	**Není zač.** [nɛni: zatʃ]
Any time.	**Je mi potěšením.** [jɛ mɪ poteʃɛni:m]
My pleasure.	**S radostí.** [s radosti:]
Forget it.	**To nestojí za řeč.** [to nɛstoji: za rʒɛtʃ]
Don't worry about it.	**Tím se netrapte.** [ti:m sɛ nɛtraptɛ]

Congratulations. Best wishes

Congratulations!
Blahopřeju!
[blahoprʒɛju!]

Happy birthday!
Všechno nejlepší k narozeninám!
[vʃɛxno nɛjlɛpʃi: k narozɛnɪna:m!]

Merry Christmas!
Veselé Vánoce!
[vɛsɛlɛ: va:notsɛ!]

Happy New Year!
Šťastný nový rok!
[ʃtʲastni: novi: rok!]

Happy Easter!
Veselé Velikonoce!
[vɛsɛlɛ: vɛlɪkonotsɛ!]

Happy Hanukkah!
Šťastnou Chanuku!
[ʃtʲastnou xanuku!]

I'd like to propose a toast.
Chtěl /Chtěla/ bych pronést přípitek.
[xtel /xtela/ bɪx pronɛ:st prʒi:pɪtɛk]

Cheers!
Na zdraví!
[na zdravi:!]

Let's drink to ...!
Pojďme se napít na ...!
[pojdʲmɛ sɛ napi:t na ...!]

To our success!
Na náš úspěch!
[na na:ʃ u:spex!]

To your success!
Na váš úspěch!
[na va:ʃ u:spex!]

Good luck!
Hodně štěstí!
[hodne ʃtesti:!]

Have a nice day!
Hezký den!
[hɛski: dɛn!]

Have a good holiday!
Hezkou dovolenou!
[hɛskou dovolɛnou!]

Have a safe journey!
Šťastnou cestu!
[ʃtʲastnou tsɛstu!]

I hope you get better soon!
Doufám, že se brzy uzdravíte!
[doufa:m, ʒe sɛ brzɪ uzdravi:tɛ!]

Socializing

Why are you sad?	**Proč jste smutný /smutná/?** [protʃ jstɛ smutni: /smutna:/?]
Smile! Cheer up!	**Usmějte se! Hlavu vzhůru!** [usmnejtɛ sɛ! hlavu vzhu:ru!]
Are you free tonight?	**Máte dnes večer čas?** [ma:tɛ dnɛs vɛtʃɛr tʃas?]
May I offer you a drink?	**Můžu vám nabídnout něco k pití?** [mu:ʒu va:m nabi:dnout netso k pɪti:?]
Would you like to dance?	**Smím prosít?** [smi:m prosi:t?]
Let's go to the movies.	**Nechcete jít do kina?** [nɛxtsɛtɛ ji:t do kɪna?]
May I invite you to ...?	**Můžu vás pozvat ...?** [mu:ʒu va:s pozvat ...?]
a restaurant	**do restaurace** [do rɛstauratsɛ]
the movies	**do kina** [do kɪna]
the theater	**do divadla** [do dɪvadla]
go for a walk	**na procházku** [na proxa:sku]
At what time?	**V kolik hodin?** [v kolɪk hodɪn?]
tonight	**dnes večer** [dnɛs vɛtʃɛr]
at six	**v šest** [v ʃɛst]
at seven	**v sedm** [v sɛdm]
at eight	**v osm** [v osm]
at nine	**v devět** [v dɛvet]
Do you like it here?	**Líbí se vám tady?** [li:bi: sɛ va:m tadɪ?]
Are you here with someone?	**Jste tady s někým?** [jstɛ tadɪ s neki:m?]
I'm with my friend.	**Jsem tady s přítelem /přítelkyní/.** [jsɛm tadɪ s prʒi:tɛlɛm /prʒi:tɛlkɪni:/]

I'm with my friends.	**Jsem tady s přáteli.**
	[jsɛm tadɪ s prʒaːtɛlɪ]
No, I'm alone.	**Ne, jsem tady sám /sama/.**
	[nɛ, jsɛm tadɪ saːm /sama/]

Do you have a boyfriend?	**Máš přítele?**
	[maːʃ prʃiːtɛlɛ?]
I have a boyfriend.	**Mám přítele.**
	[maːm prʃiːtɛlɛ]
Do you have a girlfriend?	**Máš přítelkyni?**
	[maːʃ prʃiːtɛlkɪnɪ?]
I have a girlfriend.	**Mám přítelkyni.**
	[maːm prʃiːtɛlkɪnɪ]

Can I see you again?	**Můžu tě zase vidět?**
	[muːʒu te zasɛ vɪdet?]
Can I call you?	**Můžu ti zavolat?**
	[muːʒu tɪ zavolat?]
Call me. (Give me a call.)	**Zavolej mi.**
	[zavolɛj mɪ]
What's your number?	**Jaké je tvoje číslo?**
	[jakɛː jɛ tvojɛ tʃiːslo?]
I miss you.	**Stýská se mi po tobě.**
	[stiːskaː sɛ mɪ po tobe]

You have a beautiful name.	**Máte krásné jméno.**
	[maːtɛ kraːsnɛː jmɛːno]
I love you.	**Miluju tě.**
	[mɪluju te]
Will you marry me?	**Vezmeš si mě?**
	[vɛzmɛʃ sɪ mne?]
You're kidding!	**Děláte si legraci!**
	[delaːtɛ sɪ lɛgratsɪ!]
I'm just kidding.	**Žertoval /Žertovala/ jsem.**
	[ʒertoval /ʒertovala/ jsɛm]

Are you serious?	**Myslíte to vážně?**
	[mɪsliːtɛ to vaːʒne?]
I'm serious.	**Myslím to vážně.**
	[mɪsliːm to vaːʒne]
Really?!	**Opravdu?!**
	[opravdu?!]
It's unbelievable!	**To je neuvěřitelné!**
	[to jɛ nɛuverʒɪtɛlnɛː!]
I don't believe you.	**Nevěřím vám.**
	[nɛverʒiːm vaːm]
I can't.	**Nemůžu.**
	[nɛmuːʒu]
I don't know.	**Nevím.**
	[nɛviːm]
I don't understand you.	**Nerozumím vám.**
	[nɛrozumiːm vaːm]

Please go away.

Odejděte prosím.
[odɛjdetɛ prosi:m]

Leave me alone!

Nechte mě na pokoji!
[nɛxtɛ mne na pokojɪ!]

I can't stand him.

Nesnáším ho.
[nɛsna:ʃi:m ho]

You are disgusting!

Jste odporný!
[jstɛ otporni:!]

I'll call the police!

Zavolám policii!
[zavola:m polɪtsɪjɪ!]

Sharing impressions. Emotions

I like it.	**Líbí se mi to.** [li:bi: sɛ mɪ to]
Very nice.	**Moc pěkné.** [mots peknɛ:]
That's great!	**To je skvělé!** [to jɛ skvelɛ:!]
It's not bad.	**To není špatné.** [to nɛni: ʃpatnɛ:]

I don't like it.	**Nelíbí se mi to.** [nɛli:bi: sɛ mɪ to]
It's not good.	**To není dobře.** [to nɛni: dobrʒɛ]
It's bad.	**To je špatné.** [to jɛ ʃpatnɛ:]
It's very bad.	**Je to moc špatné.** [jɛ to mots ʃpatnɛ:]
It's disgusting.	**To je odporné.** [to jɛ otpornɛ:]

I'm happy.	**Jsem šťastný /šťastná/.** [jsɛm ʃtʲastni: /ʃtʲastna:/]
I'm content.	**Jsem spokojený /spokojená/.** [jsɛm spokojɛni: /spokojɛna:/]
I'm in love.	**Jsem zamilovaný /zamilovaná/.** [jsɛm zamɪlovani: /zamɪlovana:/]
I'm calm.	**Jsem klidný /klidná/.** [jsɛm klɪdni: /klɪdna:/]
I'm bored.	**Nudím se.** [nudi:m sɛ]

I'm tired.	**Jsem unavený /unavená/.** [jsɛm unavɛni: /unavɛna:/]
I'm sad.	**Jsem smutný /smutná/.** [jsɛm smutni: /smutna:/]
I'm frightened.	**Jsem vystrašený /vystrašená/.** [jsɛm vɪstraʃɛni: /vɪstraʃɛna:/]

I'm angry.	**Zlobím se.** [zlobi:m sɛ]
I'm worried.	**Mám starosti.** [ma:m starostɪ]
I'm nervous.	**Jsem nervózní.** [jsɛm nɛrvózni:]

I'm jealous. (envious)

Žárlím.
[ʒaːrliːm]

I'm surprised.

Jsem překvapený /překvapená/.
[jsɛm prʒɛkvapɛni: /prʒɛkvapɛna:/]

I'm perplexed.

Jsem zmatený /zmatená/.
[jsɛm zmatɛni: /zmatɛna:/]

Problems. Accidents

I've got a problem.

Mám problém.
[ma:m problɛ:m]

We've got a problem.

Máme problém.
[ma:mɛ problɛ:m]

I'm lost.

Ztratil /Ztratila/ jsem se.
[stratɪl /stratɪla/ jsɛm sɛ]

I missed the last bus (train).

Zmeškal /Zmeškala/ jsem poslední autobus (vlak).
[zmɛʃkal /zmɛʃkala/ jsɛm poslɛdni: autobus (vlak)]

I don't have any money left.

Už nemám žádné peníze.
[uʒ nɛma:m ʒa:dnɛ: pɛni:zɛ]

I've lost my ...

Ztratil /Ztratila/ jsem ...
[stratɪl /stratɪla/ jsɛm ...]

Someone stole my ...

Někdo mi ukradl ...
[nɛgdo mɪ ukradl ...]

passport

pas
[pas]

wallet

peněženku
[pɛneʒeŋku]

papers

dokumenty
[dokumɛntɪ]

ticket

vstupenku
[vstupeŋku]

money

peníze
[pɛni:zɛ]

handbag

kabelku
[kabɛlku]

camera

fotoaparát
[fotoapara:t]

laptop

počítač
[potʃi:tatʃ]

tablet computer

tablet
[tablɛt]

mobile phone

mobilní telefon
[mobɪlni: tɛlɛfon]

Help me!

Pomozte mi!
[pomoztɛ mɪ!]

What's happened?

Co se stalo?
[tso sɛ stalo?]

fire	**požár** [poʒaːr]
shooting	**střelba** [strʒɛlba]
murder	**vražda** [vraʒda]
explosion	**výbuch** [viːbux]
fight	**rvačka** [rvatʃka]

Call the police!	**Zavolejte policii!** [zavolɛjtɛ polɪtsɪjɪ!]
Please hurry up!	**Pospěšte si prosím!** [pospeʃtɛ sɪ prosiːm!]
I'm looking for the police station.	**Hledám policejní stanici.** [hlɛdaːm polɪtsɛjniː stanɪtsɪ]
I need to make a call.	**Potřebuju si zavolat.** [potrʒɛbuju sɪ zavolat]
May I use your phone?	**Můžu si od vás zavolat?** [muːʒu sɪ od vaːs zavolat?]

I've been ...	**Byl /Byla/ jsem ...** [bɪl /bɪla/ jsɛm ...]
mugged	**přepaden /přepadena/** [prʃɛpadɛn /prʃɛpadɛna/]
robbed	**oloupen /oloupena/** [oloupɛn /oloupɛna/]
raped	**znásilněna** [znaːsɪlnena]
attacked (beaten up)	**napaden /napadena/** [napadɛn /napadɛna/]

Are you all right?	**Jste v pořádku?** [jstɛ v porʒaːtku?]
Did you see who it was?	**Viděl /Viděla/ jste, kdo to byl?** [vɪdel /vɪdela/ jstɛ, gdo to bɪl?]
Would you be able to recognize the person?	**Poznal /Poznala/ byste toho člověka?** [poznal /poznala/ bɪstɛ toho tʃloveka?]
Are you sure?	**Jste si tím jist /jista/?** [jstɛ sɪ tiːm jɪst /jɪsta/?]

Please calm down.	**Uklidněte se, prosím.** [uklɪdnetɛ sɛ, prosiːm]
Take it easy!	**Uklidněte se!** [uklɪdnetɛ sɛ!]
Don't worry!	**Nebojte se!** [nɛbojtɛ sɛ!]
Everything will be fine.	**Všechno bude v pořádku.** [vʃɛxno budɛ v porʒaːtku]
Everything's all right.	**Vše v pořádku.** [vʃɛ v porʒaːtku]

Come here, please.

I have some questions for you.

Wait a moment, please.

Do you have any I.D.?

Thanks. You can leave now.

Hands behind your head!

You're under arrest!

Pojďte sem, prosím.
[pojdⁱtɛ sɛm, prosiːm]

Mám na vás několik otázek.
[maːm na vaːs nekolɪk otaːzɛk]

Okamžik, prosím.
[okamʒɪk, prosiːm]

Máte nějaký průkaz totožnosti?
[maːtɛ nejaki: pruːkaz totoʒnostɪ?]

Díky. Teď můžete odejít.
[diːkɪ. tɛdⁱ muːʒetɛ odɛjiːt]

Ruce za hlavu!
[rutsɛ za hlavu!]

Jste zatčen /zatčena/!
[jstɛ zattʃɛn /zattʃɛna/!]

Health problems

Please help me.	**Prosím vás, pomozte mi.** [prosi:m va:s, pomoztɛ mɪ]
I don't feel well.	**Necítím se dobře.** [nɛtsi:ti:m sɛ dobrʒɛ]
My husband doesn't feel well.	**Můj manžel se necítí dobře.** [mu:j manʒel sɛ nɛtsi:ti: dobrʒe]
My son ...	**Můj syn ...** [mu:j sɪn ...]
My father ...	**Můj otec ...** [mu:j otɛts ...]
My wife doesn't feel well.	**Moje manželka se necítí dobře.** [mojɛ manʒelka sɛ nɛtsi:ti: dobrʒe]
My daughter ...	**Moje dcera ...** [mojɛ dtsɛra ...]
My mother ...	**Moje matka ...** [mojɛ matka ...]
I've got a ...	**Bolí mě ...** [boli: mne ...]
headache	**hlava** [hlava]
sore throat	**v krku** [v krku]
stomach ache	**žaludek** [ʒaludɛk]
toothache	**zub** [zup]
I feel dizzy.	**Mám závratě.** [ma:m za:vrate]
He has a fever.	**On má horečku.** [on ma: horɛtʃku]
She has a fever.	**Ona má horečku.** [ona ma: horɛtʃku]
I can't breathe.	**Nemůžu dýchat.** [nɛmu:ʒu di:xat]
I'm short of breath.	**Nemůžu se nadechnout.** [nɛmu:ʒu sɛ nadɛxnout]
I am asthmatic.	**Jsem astmatik /astmatička/.** [jsɛm astmatɪk /astmatɪtʃka/]
I am diabetic.	**Jsem diabetik /diabetička/.** [jsɛm dɪabɛtɪk /dɪabɛtɪtʃka/]

I can't sleep.

Nemůžu spát.
[nɛmuːʒu spaːt]

food poisoning

otrava z jídla
[otrava z jiːdla]

It hurts here.

Tady to bolí.
[tadɪ to boliː]

Help me!

Pomozte mi!
[pomoztɛ mɪ!]

I am here!

Tady jsem!
[tadɪ jsɛm!]

We are here!

Tady jsme!
[tadɪ jsmɛ!]

Get me out of here!

Dostaňte mě odtud!
[dostanʲtɛ mne odtut!]

I need a doctor.

Potřebuju doktora.
[potrʒɛbuju doktora]

I can't move.

Nemůžu se hýbat.
[nɛmuːʒu sɛ hiːbat]

I can't move my legs.

Nemůžu hýbat nohama.
[nɛmuːʒu hiːbat nohama]

I have a wound.

Jsem zraněný /zraněná/.
[jsɛm zraneniː /zranena:/]

Is it serious?

Je to vážné?
[jɛ to vaːʒnɛ:?]

My documents are in my pocket.

Doklady mám v kapse.
[dokladɪ maːm v kapsɛ]

Calm down!

Uklidněte se!
[uklɪdnetɛ sɛ!]

May I use your phone?

Můžu si od vás zavolat?
[muːʒu sɪ od vaːs zavolat?]

Call an ambulance!

Zavolejte sanitku!
[zavolɛjtɛ sanɪtku!]

It's urgent!

Je to urgentní!
[jɛ to urgɛntni:!]

It's an emergency!

To je pohotovost!
[to jɛ pohotovost!]

Please hurry up!

Prosím vás, pospěšte si!
[prosiːm vaːs, pospɛʃtɛ sɪ!]

Would you please call a doctor?

Zavolal /Zavolala/ byste prosím lékaře?
[zavolal /zavolala/ bɪstɛ prosiːm lɛːkarʒɛ?]

Where is the hospital?

Kde je nemocnice?
[gdɛ jɛ nɛmotsnɪtsɛ?]

How are you feeling?

Jak se cítíte?
[jak sɛ tsiːtiːtɛ?]

Are you all right?

Jste v pořádku?
[jstɛ v porʒaːtku?]

What's happened?	**Co se stalo?** [tso sɛ stalo?]
I feel better now.	**Teď už se cítím líp.** [tɛdʲ uʒ sɛ tsi:ti:m li:p]
It's OK.	**To je v pořádku.** [to jɛ v porʒaːtku]
It's all right.	**To je v pořádku.** [to jɛ v porʒaːtku]

At the pharmacy

pharmacy (drugstore)	**lékárna** [lɛːkaːrna]
24-hour pharmacy	**non-stop lékárna** [non-stop lɛːkaːrna]
Where is the closest pharmacy?	**Kde je nejbližší lékárna?** [gdɛ jɛ nɛjblɪʒʃiː leːkaːrna?]

Is it open now?	**Mají teď otevřeno?** [majiː tɛdʲ otɛvrʒɛno?]
At what time does it open?	**V kolik hodin otvírají?** [v kolɪk hodɪn otviːrajiː?]
At what time does it close?	**V kolik hodin zavírají?** [v kolɪk hodɪn zaviːrajiː?]

Is it far?	**Je to daleko?** [jɛ to dalɛko?]
Can I get there on foot?	**Dostanu se tam pěšky?** [dostanu sɛ tam pɛʃkɪ?]
Can you show me on the map?	**Můžete mi to ukázat na mapě?** [muːʒetɛ mɪ to ukaːzat na mape?]

Please give me something for ...	**Můžete mi prosím vás dát něco na ...** [muːʒetɛ mɪ prosiːm vaːs daːt netso na]
a headache	**bolení hlavy** [bolɛniː hlavɪ]
a cough	**kašel** [kaʃɛl]
a cold	**nachlazení** [naxlazɛniː]
the flu	**chřipka** [xrʃɪpka]

a fever	**horečka** [horɛtʃka]
a stomach ache	**bolesti v žaludku** [bolɛstɪ v ʒalutku]
nausea	**nucení na zvracení** [nutsɛniː na zvratsɛniː]
diarrhea	**průjem** [pruːjɛm]
constipation	**zácpa** [zaːtspa]

pain in the back	**bolest v zádech** [bolɛst v zaːdɛx]
chest pain	**bolest na hrudi** [bolɛst na hrudɪ]
side stitch	**boční steh** [botʃniː stɛh]
abdominal pain	**bolest břicha** [bolɛst brʒɪxa]

pill	**pilulka** [pɪlulka]
ointment, cream	**mast, krém** [mast, krɛːm]
syrup	**sirup** [sɪrup]
spray	**sprej** [sprɛj]
drops	**kapky** [kapkɪ]

You need to go to the hospital.	**Musíte jít do nemocnice.** [musiːtɛ jiːt do nɛmotsnɪtsɛ]
health insurance	**zdravotní pojištění** [zdravotniː pojɪʃteni:]
prescription	**předpis** [prʃɛtpɪs]
insect repellant	**repelent proti hmyzu** [rɛpɛlɛnt protɪ hmɪzu]
Band Aid	**náplast** [naːplast]

The bare minimum

Excuse me, ...	**Promiňte, ...** [promɪnˈtɛ, ...]
Hello.	**Dobrý den.** [dobriː dɛn]
Thank you.	**Děkuji.** [dekujɪ]
Good bye.	**Na shledanou.** [na sxlɛdanou]
Yes.	**Ano.** [ano]
No.	**Ne.** [nɛ]
I don't know.	**Nevím.** [nɛviːm]
Where? | Where to? | When?	**Kde? | Kam? | Kdy?** [gdɛ? | kam? | gdɪ?]
I need ...	**Potřebuju ...** [potrʒɛbuju ...]
I want ...	**Chci ...** [xtsɪ ...]
Do you have ...?	**Máte ...?** [maːtɛ ...?]
Is there a ... here?	**Je tady ...?** [jɛ tadɪ ...?]
May I ...?	**Můžu ...?** [muːʒu ...?]
..., please (polite request)	**..., prosím** [..., prosiːm]
I'm looking for ...	**Hledám ...** [hlɛdaːm ...]
the restroom	**toaletu** [toalɛtu]
an ATM	**bankomat** [baŋkomat]
a pharmacy (drugstore)	**lékárnu** [lɛːkaːrnu]
a hospital	**nemocnici** [nɛmotsnɪtsɪ]
the police station	**policejní stanici** [polɪtsɛjniː stanɪtsɪ]
the subway	**metro** [mɛtro]

a taxi	**taxík** [taksi:k]
the train station	**vlakové nádraží** [vlakovɛ: naːdraʒiː]

My name is ...	**Jmenuju se ...** [jmɛnuju sɛ ...]
What's your name?	**Jak se jmenujete?** [jak sɛ jmɛnujɛtɛ?]
Could you please help me?	**Můžete mi prosím pomoct?** [muːʒetɛ mɪ prosiːm pomotst?]
I've got a problem.	**Mám problém.** [maːm problɛːm]
I don't feel well.	**Necítím se dobře.** [nɛtsiːtiːm sɛ dobrʒɛ]
Call an ambulance!	**Zavolejte sanitku!** [zavolɛjtɛ sanɪtku!]
May I make a call?	**Můžu si zavolat?** [muːʒu sɪ zavolat?]

I'm sorry.	**Omlouvám se.** [omlouvaːm sɛ]
You're welcome.	**Není zač.** [nɛniː zatʃ]

I, me	**Já** [jaː]
you (inform.)	**ty** [tɪ]
he	**on** [on]
she	**ona** [ona]
they (masc.)	**oni** [onɪ]
they (fem.)	**ony** [onɪ]
we	**my** [mɪ]
you (pl)	**vy** [vɪ]
you (sg, form.)	**vy** [vɪ]

ENTRANCE	**VCHOD** [vxot]
EXIT	**VÝCHOD** [viːxot]
OUT OF ORDER	**MIMO PROVOZ** [mɪmo provos]
CLOSED	**ZAVŘENO** [zavrʒɛno]

OPEN

OTEVŘENO
[otɛvrʒɛno]

FOR WOMEN

ŽENY
[ʒenɪ]

FOR MEN

MUŽI
[muʒɪ]

TOPICAL VOCABULARY

This section contains more than 3,000 of the most important words.
The dictionary will provide invaluable assistance while traveling abroad, because frequently individual words are enough for you to be understood.
The dictionary includes a convenient transcription of each foreign word

T&P Books Publishing

VOCABULARY
CONTENTS

T&P Books Publishing

BASIC CONCEPTS

T&P Books Publishing

I, me	já	[ja:]
you	ty	[tɪ]

he	on	[on]
she	ona	[ona]

we	my	[mɪ]
you (to a group)	vy	[vɪ]
they (inanim.)	ony	[onɪ]
they (anim.)	oni	[onɪ]

2. Greetings. Salutations

Hello! (fam.)	Dobrý den!	[dobri: dɛn]
Hello! (form.)	Dobrý den!	[dobri: dɛn]
Good morning!	Dobré jitro!	[dobrɛ: jɪtro]
Good afternoon!	Dobrý den!	[dobri: dɛn]
Good evening!	Dobrý večer!	[dobri: vɛtʃɛr]

to say hello	zdravit	[zdravɪt]
Hi! (hello)	Ahoj!	[ahoj]
greeting (n)	pozdrav (m)	[pozdraf]
to greet (vt)	zdravit	[zdravɪt]
How are you?	Jak se máte?	[jak sɛ ma:tɛ]
What's new?	Co je nového?	[tso jɛ novɛ:ho]

Bye-Bye! Goodbye!	Na shledanou!	[na sxlɛdanou]
See you soon!	Brzy na shledanou!	[brzɪ na sxlɛdanou]
Farewell!	Sbohem!	[zbohɛm]
to say goodbye	loučit se	[loutʃɪt sɛ]
So long!	Ahoj!	[ahoj]

Thank you!	Děkuji!	[dekujɪ]
Thank you very much!	Děkuji mnohokrát!	[dekujɪ mnohokra:t]
You're welcome	Prosím	[prosi:m]
Don't mention it!	Nemoci se dočkat	[nɛmotsɪ sɛ dotʃkat]
It was nothing	Není zač	[nɛni: zatʃ]

Excuse me! (fam.)	Promiň!	[promɪɲ]
Excuse me! (form.)	Promiňte!	[promɪɲtɛ]
to excuse (forgive)	omlouvat	[omlouvat]
to apologize (vi)	omlouvat se	[omlouvat sɛ]

My apologies	Má soustrast	[ma: soustrast]
I'm sorry!	Promiňte!	[promɪnʲtɛ]
to forgive (vt)	omlouvat	[omlouvat]
please (adv)	prosím	[prosi:m]

Don't forget!	Nezapomeňte!	[nɛzapomɛnʲtɛ]
Certainly!	Jistě!	[jɪste]
Of course not!	Rozhodně ne!	[rozhodne nɛ]
Okay! (I agree)	Souhlasím!	[souhlasi:m]
That's enough!	Dost!	[dost]

3. Questions

Who?	Kdo?	[gdo]
What?	Co?	[tso]
Where? (at, in)	Kde?	[gdɛ]
Where (to)?	Kam?	[kam]
From where?	Odkud?	[otkut]
When?	Kdy?	[gdɪ]
Why? (What for?)	Proč?	[protʃ]
Why? (~ are you crying?)	Proč?	[protʃ]

What for?	Na co?	[na tso]
How? (in what way)	Jak?	[jak]
What? (What kind of …?)	Jaký?	[jaki:]
Which?	Který?	[ktɛri:]

To whom?	Komu?	[komu]
About whom?	O kom?	[o kom]
About what?	O čem?	[o tʃɛm]
With whom?	S kým?	[s ki:m]

| How many? How much? | Kolik? | [kolɪk] |
| Whose? | Čí? | [tʃi:] |

4. Prepositions

with (accompanied by)	s, se	[s], [sɛ]
without	bez	[bɛz]
to (indicating direction)	do	[do]
about (talking ~ …)	o	[o]
before (in time)	před	[prʃɛt]
in front of …	před	[prʃɛt]

under (beneath, below)	pod	[pot]
above (over)	nad	[nat]
on (atop)	na	[na]
from (off, out of)	z	[z]

of (made from)	z	[z]
in (e.g., ~ ten minutes)	za	[za]
over (across the top of)	přes	[prʃɛs]

5. Function words. Adverbs. Part 1

Where? (at, in)	Kde?	[gdɛ]
here (adv)	zde	[zdɛ]
there (adv)	tam	[tam]

| somewhere (to be) | někde | [negdɛ] |
| nowhere (not in any place) | nikde | [nɪgdɛ] |

| by (near, beside) | u ... | [u] |
| by the window | u okna | [u okna] |

Where (to)?	Kam?	[kam]
here (e.g., come ~!)	sem	[sɛm]
there (e.g., to go ~)	tam	[tam]
from here (adv)	odsud	[otsut]
from there (adv)	odtamtud	[odtamtut]

| close (adv) | blízko | [bli:sko] |
| far (adv) | daleko | [dalɛko] |

near (e.g., ~ Paris)	kolem	[kolɛm]
nearby (adv)	poblíž	[pobli:ʒ]
not far (adv)	nedaleko	[nɛdalɛko]

left (adj)	levý	[lɛvi:]
on the left	zleva	[zlɛva]
to the left	vlevo	[vlɛvo]

right (adj)	pravý	[pravi:]
on the right	zprava	[sprava]
to the right	vpravo	[vpravo]

in front (adv)	zpředu	[sprʃɛdu]
front (as adj)	přední	[prʃɛdni:]
ahead (the kids ran ~)	vpřed	[vprʃɛt]

behind (adv)	za	[za]
from behind	zezadu	[zɛzadu]
back (towards the rear)	zpět	[spet]

| middle | střed (m) | [strʃɛt] |
| in the middle | uprostřed | [uprostrʃɛt] |

| at the side | z boku | [z boku] |
| everywhere (adv) | všude | [vʃudɛ] |

around (in all directions)	kolem	[kolɛm]
from inside	zevnitř	[zɛvnɪtrʃ]
somewhere (to go)	někam	[nekam]
straight (directly)	přímo	[prʃi:mo]
back (e.g., come ~)	zpět	[spet]

from anywhere	odněkud	[odnekut]
from somewhere	odněkud	[odnekut]

firstly (adv)	za prvé	[za prvɛ:]
secondly (adv)	za druhé	[za druhɛ:]
thirdly (adv)	za třetí	[za trʃɛti:]

suddenly (adv)	najednou	[najɛdnou]
at first (in the beginning)	zpočátku	[spotʃa:tku]
for the first time	poprvé	[poprvɛ:]
long before ...	dávno před ...	[da:vno prʃɛt]
anew (over again)	znovu	[znovu]
for good (adv)	navždy	[navʒdɪ]

never (adv)	nikdy	[nɪgdɪ]
again (adv)	opět	[opet]
now (at present)	nyní	[nɪni:]
often (adv)	často	[tʃasto]
then (adv)	tehdy	[tɛhdɪ]
urgently (quickly)	neodkladně	[nɛotkladne]
usually (adv)	obyčejně	[obɪtʃɛjne]

by the way, ...	mimochodem	[mɪmoxodɛm]
possibly	možná	[moʒna:]
probably (adv)	asi	[asɪ]
maybe (adv)	možná	[moʒna:]
besides ...	kromě toho ...	[kromne toho]
that's why ...	proto ...	[proto]
in spite of ...	nehledě na ...	[nɛhlɛde na]
thanks to ...	díky ...	[di:kɪ]

what (pron.)	co	[tso]
that (conj.)	že	[ʒe]
something	něco	[netso]
anything (something)	něco	[netso]
nothing	nic	[nɪts]

who (pron.)	kdo	[gdo]
someone	někdo	[negdo]
somebody	někdo	[negdo]

nobody	nikdo	[nɪgdo]
nowhere (a voyage to ~)	nikam	[nɪkam]
nobody's	ničí	[nɪtʃi:]
somebody's	něčí	[netʃi:]
so (I'm ~ glad)	tak	[tak]

also (as well)	také	[takɛ:]
too (as well)	také	[takɛ:]

6. Function words. Adverbs. Part 2

Why?	Proč?	[protʃ]
for some reason	z nějakých důvodů	[z nejaki:x du:vodu:]
because ...	protože ...	[protoʒe]
for some purpose	z nějakých důvodů	[z nejaki:x du:vodu:]

and	a	[a]
or	nebo	[nɛbo]
but	ale	[alɛ]
for (e.g., ~ me)	pro	[pro]

too (~ many people)	příliš	[prʃi:lɪʃ]
only (exclusively)	jenom	[jɛnom]
exactly (adv)	přesně	[prʃɛsne]
about (more or less)	kolem	[kolɛm]

approximately (adv)	přibližně	[prʃɪblɪʒne]
approximate (adj)	přibližný	[prʃɪblɪʒni:]
almost (adv)	skoro	[skoro]
the rest	zbytek (m)	[zbɪtɛk]

the other (second)	druhý	[druhi:]
other (different)	jiný	[jɪni:]
each (adj)	každý	[kaʒdi:]
any (no matter which)	každý	[kaʒdi:]
many, much (a lot of)	mnoho	[mnoho]
many people	mnozí	[mnozi:]
all (everyone)	všichni	[vʃɪxnɪ]

in return for ...	výměnou za ...	[vi:mnenou za]
in exchange (adv)	místo	[mi:sto]
by hand (made)	ručně	[rutʃne]
hardly (negative opinion)	sotva	[sotva]

probably (adv)	asi	[asɪ]
on purpose (intentionally)	schválně	[sxva:lne]
by accident (adv)	náhodou	[na:hodou]

very (adv)	velmi	[vɛlmɪ]
for example (adv)	například	[naprʃi:klat]
between	mezi	[mɛzɪ]
among	mezi	[mɛzɪ]
so much (such a lot)	tolik	[tolɪk]
especially (adv)	zejména	[zɛjmɛ:na]

NUMBERS.
MISCELLANEOUS

T&P Books Publishing

0 zero	**nula** (ž)	[nula]
1 one	**jeden**	[jɛdɛn]
2 two	**dva**	[dva]
3 three	**tři**	[trʃɪ]
4 four	**čtyři**	[ʧtɪrʒɪ]
5 five	**pět**	[pet]
6 six	**šest**	[ʃɛst]
7 seven	**sedm**	[sɛdm]
8 eight	**osm**	[osm]
9 nine	**devět**	[dɛvet]
10 ten	**deset**	[dɛsɛt]
11 eleven	**jedenáct**	[jɛdɛnaːʦt]
12 twelve	**dvanáct**	[dvanaːʦt]
13 thirteen	**třináct**	[trʃɪnaːʦt]
14 fourteen	**čtrnáct**	[ʧtrnaːʦt]
15 fifteen	**patnáct**	[patnaːʦt]
16 sixteen	**šestnáct**	[ʃɛstnaːʦt]
17 seventeen	**sedmnáct**	[sɛdmnaːʦt]
18 eighteen	**osmnáct**	[osmnaːʦt]
19 nineteen	**devatenáct**	[dɛvatɛnaːʦt]
20 twenty	**dvacet**	[dvaʦɛt]
21 twenty-one	**dvacet jeden**	[dvaʦɛt jɛdɛn]
22 twenty-two	**dvacet dva**	[dvaʦɛt dva]
23 twenty-three	**dvacet tři**	[dvaʦɛt trʃɪ]
30 thirty	**třicet**	[trʃɪʦɛt]
31 thirty-one	**třicet jeden**	[trʃɪʦɛt jɛdɛn]
32 thirty-two	**třicet dva**	[trʃɪʦɛt dva]
33 thirty-three	**třicet tři**	[trʃɪʦɛt trʃɪ]
40 forty	**čtyřicet**	[ʧtɪrʒɪʦɛt]
41 forty-one	**čtyřicet jeden**	[ʧtɪrʒɪʦɛt jɛdɛn]
42 forty-two	**čtyřicet dva**	[ʧtɪrʒɪʦɛt dva]
43 forty-three	**čtyřicet tři**	[ʧtɪrʒɪʦɛt trʃɪ]
50 fifty	**padesát**	[padesaːt]
51 fifty-one	**padesát jeden**	[padesaːt jɛdɛn]
52 fifty-two	**padesát dva**	[padesaːt dva]
53 fifty-three	**padesát tři**	[padesaːt trʃɪ]
60 sixty	**šedesát**	[ʃɛdɛsaːt]

61 sixty-one	šedesát jeden	[ʃɛdɛsaːt jɛdɛn]
62 sixty-two	šedesát dva	[ʃɛdɛsaːt dva]
63 sixty-three	šedesát tři	[ʃɛdɛsaːt trʃɪ]

70 seventy	sedmdesát	[sɛdmdɛsaːt
71 seventy-one	sedmdesát jeden	[sɛdmdɛsaːt jɛdɛn]
72 seventy-two	sedmdesát dva	[sɛdmdɛsaːt dva]
73 seventy-three	sedmdesát tři	[sɛdmdɛsaːt trʃɪ]

80 eighty	osmdesát	[osmdɛsaːt
81 eighty-one	osmdesát jeden	[osmdɛsaːt jɛdɛn]
82 eighty-two	osmdesát dva	[osmdɛsaːt dva]
83 eighty-three	osmdesát tři	[osmdɛsaːt trʃɪ]

90 ninety	devadesát	[dɛvadɛsaːt
91 ninety-one	devadesát jeden	[dɛvadɛsaːt jɛdɛn]
92 ninety-two	devadesát dva	[dɛvadɛsaːt dva]
93 ninety-three	devadesát tři	[dɛvadɛsaːt trʃɪ]

8. Cardinal numbers. Part 2

100 one hundred	sto	[sto]
200 two hundred	dvě stě	[dve ste]
300 three hundred	tři sta	[trʃɪ sta]
400 four hundred	čtyři sta	[ʧtɪrʒɪ sta]
500 five hundred	pět set	[pet sɛt]

600 six hundred	šest set	[ʃɛst sɛt]
700 seven hundred	sedm set	[sɛdm sɛt]
800 eight hundred	osm set	[osm sɛt]
900 nine hundred	devět set	[dɛvet sɛt]

1000 one thousand	tisíc (m)	[tɪsiːʦ]
2000 two thousand	dva tisíce	[dva tɪsiːʦɛ]
3000 three thousand	tři tisíce	[trʃɪ tɪsiːʦɛ]
10000 ten thousand	deset tisíc	[dɛsɛt tɪsiːʦ]
one hundred thousand	sto tisíc	[sto tɪsiːʦ]
million	milión (m)	[mɪlɪoːn]
billion	miliarda (ž)	[mɪlɪarda]

9. Ordinal numbers

first (adj)	první	[prvniː]
second (adj)	druhý	[druhiː]
third (adj)	třetí	[trʃɛtiː]
fourth (adj)	čtvrtý	[ʧtvrtiː]
fifth (adj)	pátý	[paːtiː]
sixth (adj)	šestý	[ʃɛstiː]

seventh (adj)	**sedmý**	[sɛdmiː]
eighth (adj)	**osmý**	[osmiː]
ninth (adj)	**devátý**	[dɛvaːtiː]
tenth (adj)	**desátý**	[dɛsaːtiː]

COLOURS. UNITS OF MEASUREMENT

T&P Books Publishing

10. Colors

color	**barva** (ž)	[barva]
shade (tint)	**odstín** (m)	[otsti:n]
hue	**tón** (m)	[to:n]
rainbow	**duha** (ž)	[duha]

white (adj)	**bílý**	[bi:li:]
black (adj)	**černý**	[ʧɛrni:]
gray (adj)	**šedý**	[ʃɛdi:]

green (adj)	**zelený**	[zɛlɛni:]
yellow (adj)	**žlutý**	[ʒluti:]
red (adj)	**červený**	[ʧɛrvɛni:]
blue (adj)	**modrý**	[modri:]
light blue (adj)	**bledě modrý**	[blɛde modri:]
pink (adj)	**růžový**	[ru:ʒovi:]
orange (adj)	**oranžový**	[oranʒovi:]
violet (adj)	**fialový**	[fɪalovi:]
brown (adj)	**hnědý**	[hnedi:]

golden (adj)	**zlatý**	[zlati:]
silvery (adj)	**stříbřitý**	[strʃi:brʒɪti:]
beige (adj)	**béžový**	[bɛ:ʒovi:]
cream (adj)	**krémový**	[krɛ:movi:]
turquoise (adj)	**tyrkysový**	[tɪrkɪsovi:]
cherry red (adj)	**višňový**	[vɪʃɲʲovi:]
lilac (adj)	**lila**	[lɪla]
crimson (adj)	**malinový**	[malɪnovi:]

light (adj)	**světlý**	[svetli:]
dark (adj)	**tmavý**	[tmavi:]
bright, vivid (adj)	**jasný**	[jasni:]

colored (pencils)	**barevný**	[barɛvni:]
color (e.g., ~ film)	**barevný**	[barɛvni:]
black-and-white (adj)	**černobílý**	[ʧɛrnobi:li:]
plain (one-colored)	**jednobarevný**	[jɛdnobarɛvni:]
multicolored (adj)	**různobarevný**	[ru:znobarɛvni:]

11. Units of measurement

weight	**váha** (ž)	[va:ha]
length	**délka** (ž)	[dɛ:lka]

width	šířka (ž)	[ʃiːrʃka]
height	výška (ž)	[viːʃka]
depth	hloubka (ž)	[hloupka]
volume	objem (m)	[objɛm]
area	plocha (ž)	[ploxa]

gram	gram (m)	[gram]
milligram	miligram (m)	[mɪlɪgram]
kilogram	kilogram (m)	[kɪlogram]
ton	tuna (ž)	[tuna]
pound	libra (ž)	[lɪbra]
ounce	unce (ž)	[unʦɛ]

meter	metr (m)	[mɛtr]
millimeter	milimetr (m)	[mɪlɪmɛtr]
centimeter	centimetr (m)	[ʦɛntɪmɛtr]
kilometer	kilometr (m)	[kɪlomɛtr]
mile	míle (ž)	[miːlɛ]

inch	coul (m)	[ʦoul]
foot	stopa (ž)	[stopa]
yard	yard (m)	[jart]

square meter	čtvereční metr (m)	[ʧtvɛrɛʧniː mɛtr]
hectare	hektar (m)	[hɛktar]
liter	litr (m)	[lɪtr]
degree	stupeň (m)	[stupɛnʲ]
volt	volt (m)	[volt]
ampere	ampér (m)	[ampɛːr]
horsepower	koňská síla (ž)	[konʲska: siːla]

quantity	množství (s)	[mnoʒstviː]
a little bit of …	trochu …	[troxu]
half	polovina (ž)	[polovɪna]
dozen	tucet (m)	[tuʦɛt]
piece (item)	kus (m)	[kus]

| size | rozměr (m) | [rozmner] |
| scale (map ~) | měřítko (s) | [mnerʒiːtko] |

minimal (adj)	minimální	[mɪnɪmaːlniː]
the smallest (adj)	nejmenší	[nɛjmɛnʃiː]
medium (adj)	střední	[strʃɛdniː]
maximal (adj)	maximální	[maksɪmaːlniː]
the largest (adj)	největší	[nɛjvɛtʃiː]

12. Containers

| canning jar (glass ~) | sklenice (ž) | [sklɛnɪʦɛ] |
| can | plechovka (ž) | [plɛxofka] |

bucket	**vědro** (s)	[vedro]
barrel	**sud** (m)	[sut]
wash basin (e.g., plastic ~)	**mísa** (ž)	[mi:sa]
tank (100L water ~)	**nádrž** (ž)	[na:drʃ]
hip flask	**plochá láhev** (ž)	[ploxa: la:gɛf]
jerrycan	**kanystr** (m)	[kanɪstr]
tank (e.g., tank car)	**cisterna** (ž)	[ʦɪstɛrna]
mug	**hrníček** (m)	[hrni:ʧɛk]
cup (of coffee, etc.)	**šálek** (m)	[ʃa:lɛk]
saucer	**talířek** (m)	[tali:rʒɛk]
glass (tumbler)	**sklenice** (ž)	[sklɛnɪʦɛ]
wine glass	**sklenka** (ž)	[sklɛŋka]
stock pot (soup pot)	**hrnec** (m)	[hrnɛʦ]
bottle (~ of wine)	**láhev** (ž)	[la:hɛf]
neck (of the bottle, etc.)	**hrdlo** (s)	[hrdlo]
carafe (decanter)	**karafa** (ž)	[karafa]
pitcher	**džbán** (m)	[dʒba:n]
vessel (container)	**nádoba** (ž)	[na:doba]
pot (crock, stoneware ~)	**hrnec** (m)	[hrnɛʦ]
vase	**váza** (ž)	[va:za]
flacon, bottle (perfume ~)	**flakón** (m)	[flako:n]
vial, small bottle	**lahvička** (ž)	[lahvɪʧka]
tube (of toothpaste)	**tuba** (ž)	[tuba]
sack (bag)	**pytel** (m)	[pɪtɛl]
bag (paper ~, plastic ~)	**sáček** (m)	[sa:ʧɛk]
pack (of cigarettes, etc.)	**balíček** (m)	[bali:ʧɛk]
box (e.g., shoebox)	**krabice** (ž)	[krabɪʦɛ]
crate	**schránka** (ž)	[sxra:ŋka]
basket	**koš** (m)	[koʃ]

MAIN VERBS

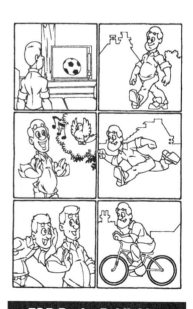

T&P Books Publishing

13. The most important verbs. Part 1

to advise (vt)	radit	[radɪt]
to agree (say yes)	souhlasit	[souhlasɪt]
to answer (vi, vt)	odpovídat	[otpovi:dat]
to apologize (vi)	omlouvat se	[omlouvat sɛ]
to arrive (vi)	přijíždět	[prʃɪji:ʒdet]
to ask (~ oneself)	ptát se	[pta:t sɛ]
to ask (~ sb to do sth)	prosit	[prosɪt]
to be (vi)	být	[bi:t]
to be afraid	bát se	[ba:t sɛ]
to be hungry	mít hlad	[mi:t hlat]
to be interested in …	zajímat se	[zaji:mat sɛ]
to be needed	být potřebný	[bi:t potrʃɛbni:]
to be surprised	divit se	[dɪvɪt sɛ]
to be thirsty	mít žízeň	[mi:t ʒi:zɛnʲ]
to begin (vt)	začínat	[zatʃi:nat]
to belong to …	patřit	[patrʃɪt]
to boast (vi)	vychloubat se	[vɪxloubat sɛ]
to break (split into pieces)	lámat	[la:mat]
to call (~ for help)	volat	[volat]
can (v aux)	moci	[motsɪ]
to catch (vt)	chytat	[xɪtat]
to change (vt)	změnit	[zmnenɪt]
to choose (select)	vybírat	[vɪbi:rat]
to come down (the stairs)	jít dolů	[ji:t dolu:]
to compare (vt)	porovnávat	[porovna:vat]
to complain (vi, vt)	stěžovat si	[steʒovat sɪ]
to confuse (mix up)	plést	[plɛ:st]
to continue (vt)	pokračovat	[pokratʃovat]
to control (vt)	kontrolovat	[kontrolovat]
to cook (dinner)	vařit	[varʒɪt]
to cost (vt)	stát	[sta:t]
to count (add up)	počítat	[potʃi:tat]
to count on …	spoléhat na …	[spolɛ:hat na]
to create (vt)	vytvořit	[vɪtvorʒɪt]
to cry (weep)	plakat	[plakat]

14. The most important verbs. Part 2

to deceive (vi, vt)	podvádět	[podva:det]
to decorate (tree, street)	zdobit	[zdobɪt]
to defend (a country, etc.)	bránit	[bra:nɪt]
to demand (request firmly)	žádat	[ʒa:dat]
to dig (vt)	rýt	[ri:t]
to discuss (vt)	projednávat	[projɛdna:vat]
to do (vt)	dělat	[delat]
to doubt (have doubts)	pochybovat	[poxɪbovat]
to drop (let fall)	pouštět	[pouʃtet]
to enter (room, house, etc.)	vcházet	[vxa:zet]
to excuse (forgive)	omlouvat	[omlouvat]
to exist (vi)	existovat	[ɛgzɪstovat]
to expect (foresee)	předvídat	[prʃɛdvi:dat]
to explain (vt)	vysvětlovat	[vɪsvetlovat]
to fall (vi)	padat	[padat]
to find (vt)	nacházet	[naxa:zɛt]
to finish (vt)	končit	[kontʃɪt]
to fly (vi)	letět	[lɛtet]
to follow ... (come after)	následovat	[na:slɛdovat]
to forget (vi, vt)	zapomínat	[zapomi:nat]
to forgive (vt)	odpouštět	[otpouʃtet]
to give (vt)	dávat	[da:vat]
to give a hint	narážet	[nara:ʒet]
to go (on foot)	jít	[ji:t]
to go for a swim	koupat se	[koupat sɛ]
to go out (for dinner, etc.)	vycházet	[vɪxa:zɛt]
to guess (the answer)	rozluštit	[rozluʃtɪt]
to have (vt)	mít	[mi:t]
to have breakfast	snídat	[sni:dat]
to have dinner	večeřet	[vɛtʃɛrʒɛt]
to have lunch	obědvat	[obedvat]
to hear (vt)	slyšet	[slɪʃɛt]
to help (vt)	pomáhat	[poma:hat]
to hide (vt)	schovávat	[sxova:vat]
to hope (vi, vt)	doufat	[doufat]
to hunt (vi, vt)	lovit	[lovɪt]
to hurry (vi)	spěchat	[spexat]

15. The most important verbs. Part 3

to inform (vt)	informovat	[ɪnformovat]
to insist (vi, vt)	trvat	[trvat]
to insult (vt)	urážet	[ura:ʒet]
to invite (vt)	zvát	[zva:t]
to joke (vi)	žertovat	[ʒertovat]

to keep (vt)	zachovávat	[zaxova:vat]
to keep silent, to hush	mlčet	[mlt͡ʃɛt]
to kill (vt)	zabíjet	[zabi:jɛt]
to know (sb)	znát	[zna:t]
to know (sth)	vědět	[vedet]
to laugh (vi)	smát se	[sma:t sɛ]

to liberate (city, etc.)	osvobozovat	[osvobozovat]
to like (I like …)	líbit se	[li:bɪt sɛ]
to look for … (search)	hledat	[hlɛdat]
to love (sb)	milovat	[mɪlovat]
to make a mistake	mýlit se	[mi:lɪt sɛ]
to manage, to run	řídit	[rʒi:dɪt]
to mean (signify)	znamenat	[znamɛnat]
to mention (talk about)	zmiňovat se	[zmɪnʲovat sɛ]
to miss (school, etc.)	zameškávat	[zameʃka:vat]
to notice (see)	všímat si	[vʃi:mat sɪ]

to object (vi, vt)	namítat	[nami:tat]
to observe (see)	pozorovat	[pozorovat]
to open (vt)	otvírat	[otvi:rat]
to order (meal, etc.)	objednávat	[objɛdna:vat]
to order (mil.)	rozkazovat	[roskazovat]
to own (possess)	vlastnit	[vlastnɪt]
to participate (vi)	zúčastnit se	[zu:t͡ʃastnɪt sɛ]
to pay (vi, vt)	platit	[platɪt]
to permit (vt)	dovolovat	[dovolovat]
to plan (vt)	plánovat	[pla:novat]
to play (children)	hrát	[hra:t]

to pray (vi, vt)	modlit se	[modlɪt sɛ]
to prefer (vt)	dávat přednost	[da:vat prʃɛdnost]
to promise (vt)	slibovat	[slɪbovat]
to pronounce (vt)	vyslovovat	[vɪslovovat]
to propose (vt)	nabízet	[nabi:zɛt]
to punish (vt)	trestat	[trɛstat]

16. The most important verbs. Part 4

| to read (vi, vt) | číst | [t͡ʃi:st] |
| to recommend (vt) | doporučovat | [doporut͡ʃovat] |

to refuse (vi, vt)	odmítat	[odmi:tat]
to regret (be sorry)	litovat	[lɪtovat]
to rent (sth from sb)	pronajímat si	[pronaji:mat sɪ]

to repeat (say again)	opakovat	[opakovat]
to reserve, to book	rezervovat	[rɛzɛrvovat]
to run (vi)	běžet	[beʒet]
to save (rescue)	zachraňovat	[zaxranʲovat]
to say (~ thank you)	říci	[rʒi:ʦɪ]

to scold (vt)	nadávat	[nada:vat]
to see (vt)	vidět	[vɪdet]
to sell (vt)	prodávat	[proda:vat]
to send (vt)	odesílat	[odɛsi:lat]
to shoot (vi)	střílet	[strʃi:lɛt]

to shout (vi)	křičet	[krʃɪtʃɛt]
to show (vt)	ukazovat	[ukazovat]
to sign (document)	podepisovat	[podɛpɪsovat]
to sit down (vi)	sednout si	[sɛdnout sɪ]

to smile (vi)	usmívat se	[usmi:vat sɛ]
to speak (vi, vt)	mluvit	[mluvɪt]
to steal (money, etc.)	krást	[kra:st]
to stop (for pause, etc.)	zastavovat se	[zastavovat sɛ]
to stop (please ~ calling me)	zastavovat	[zastavovat]

to study (vt)	studovat	[studovat]
to swim (vi)	plavat	[plavat]
to take (vt)	brát	[bra:t]
to think (vi, vt)	myslit	[mɪslɪt]
to threaten (vt)	vyhrožovat	[vɪhroʒovat]

to touch (with hands)	dotýkat se	[doti:kat sɛ]
to translate (vt)	překládat	[prʃɛkla:dat]
to trust (vt)	důvěřovat	[du:verʒovat]
to try (attempt)	zkoušet	[skouʃɛt]
to turn (e.g., ~ left)	zatáčet	[zata:tʃɛt]

to underestimate (vt)	podceňovat	[podʦɛnʲovat]
to understand (vt)	rozumět	[rozumnet]
to unite (vt)	sjednocovat	[sjɛdnoʦovat]
to wait (vt)	čekat	[tʃɛkat]

to want (wish, desire)	chtít	[xti:t]
to warn (vt)	upozorňovat	[upozornʲovat]
to work (vi)	pracovat	[praʦovat]
to write (vt)	psát	[psa:t]
to write down	zapisovat si	[zapɪsovat sɪ]

TIME. CALENDAR

T&P Books Publishing

17. Weekdays

Monday	pondělí (s)	[pondeli:]
Tuesday	úterý (s)	[u:tɛri:]
Wednesday	středa (ž)	[strʃɛda]
Thursday	čtvrtek (m)	[tʃtvrtɛk]
Friday	pátek (m)	[pa:tɛk]
Saturday	sobota (ž)	[sobota]
Sunday	neděle (ž)	[nɛdelɛ]
today (adv)	dnes	[dnɛs]
tomorrow (adv)	zítra	[zi:tra]
the day after tomorrow	pozítří	[pozi:trʃi:]
yesterday (adv)	včera	[vtʃɛra]
the day before yesterday	předevčírem	[prʃɛdɛvtʃi:rɛm]
day	den (m)	[dɛn]
working day	pracovní den (m)	[pratsovni: dɛn]
public holiday	sváteční den (m)	[sva:tɛtʃni: dɛn]
day off	volno (s)	[volno]
weekend	víkend (m)	[vi:kɛnt]
all day long	celý den	[tsɛli: dɛn]
the next day (adv)	příští den	[prʃi:ʃti: dɛn]
two days ago	před dvěma dny	[prʃɛd dvema dnɪ]
the day before	den předtím	[dɛn prʃɛdti:m]
daily (adj)	denní	[dɛnni:]
every day (adv)	denně	[dɛnne]
week	týden (m)	[ti:dɛn]
last week (adv)	minulý týden	[mɪnuli: ti:dɛn]
next week (adv)	příští týden	[prʃi:ʃti: ti:dɛn]
weekly (adj)	týdenní	[ti:dɛnni:]
every week (adv)	týdně	[ti:dne]
twice a week	dvakrát týdně	[dvakra:t ti:dne]
every Tuesday	každé úterý	[kaʒdɛ: u:tɛri:]

18. Hours. Day and night

morning	ráno (s)	[ra:no]
in the morning	ráno	[ra:no]
noon, midday	poledne (s)	[polɛdnɛ]
in the afternoon	odpoledne	[otpolɛdnɛ]
evening	večer (m)	[vɛtʃɛr]

in the evening	večer	[vɛtʃɛr]
night	noc (ž)	[nots]
at night	v noci	[v notsɪ]
midnight	půlnoc (ž)	[puːlnots]

second	sekunda (ž)	[sɛkunda]
minute	minuta (ž)	[mɪnuta]
hour	hodina (ž)	[hodɪna]
half an hour	půlhodina (ž)	[puːlhodɪna]
a quarter-hour	čtvrthodina (ž)	[tʃtvrthodɪna]
fifteen minutes	patnáct minut	[patnaːtst mɪnut]
24 hours	den a noc	[dɛn a nots]

sunrise	východ (m) slunce	[viːxod sluntsɛ]
dawn	úsvit (m)	[uːsvɪt]
early morning	časné ráno (s)	[tʃasnɛː raːno]
sunset	západ (m) slunce	[zaːpat sluntsɛ]

early in the morning	brzy ráno	[brzɪ raːno]
this morning	dnes ráno	[dnɛs raːno]
tomorrow morning	zítra ráno	[ziːtra raːno]

this afternoon	dnes odpoledne	[dnɛs otpolɛdnɛ]
in the afternoon	odpoledne	[otpolɛdnɛ]
tomorrow afternoon	zítra odpoledne	[ziːtra otpolɛdnɛ]

| tonight (this evening) | dnes večer | [dnɛs vɛtʃɛr] |
| tomorrow night | zítra večer | [ziːtra vɛtʃɛr] |

at 3 o'clock sharp	přesně ve tři hodiny	[prʃɛsnɛ vɛ trʃɪ hodɪnɪ]
about 4 o'clock	kolem čtyř hodin	[kolɛm tʃtɪrʒ hodɪn]
by 12 o'clock	do dvanácti hodin	[do dvanaːtstɪ hodɪn]

in 20 minutes	za dvacet minut	[za dvatsɛt mɪnut]
in an hour	za hodinu	[za hodɪnu]
on time (adv)	včas	[vtʃas]

a quarter to ...	tři čtvrtě	[trʃɪ tʃtvrte]
within an hour	během hodiny	[behɛm hodɪnɪ]
every 15 minutes	každých patnáct minut	[kaʒdiːx patnaːtst mɪnut]
round the clock	celodenně	[tsɛlodɛnne]

19. Months. Seasons

January	leden (m)	[lɛdɛn]
February	únor (m)	[uːnor]
March	březen (m)	[brʒɛzɛn]
April	duben (m)	[dubɛn]
May	květen (m)	[kvetɛn]
June	červen (m)	[tʃɛrvɛn]

July	červenec (m)	[ʧɛrvɛnɛʦ]
August	srpen (m)	[srpɛn]
September	září (s)	[za:rʒi:]
October	říjen (m)	[rʒi:jɛn]
November	listopad (m)	[lɪstopat]
December	prosinec (m)	[prosɪnɛʦ]

spring	jaro (s)	[jaro]
in spring	na jaře	[na jarʒɛ]
spring (as adj)	jarní	[jarni:]

summer	léto (s)	[lɛ:to]
in summer	v létě	[v lɛ:te]
summer (as adj)	letní	[lɛtni:]

fall	podzim (m)	[podzɪm]
in fall	na podzim	[na podzɪm]
fall (as adj)	podzimní	[podzɪmni:]

winter	zima (ž)	[zɪma]
in winter	v zimě	[v zɪmne]
winter (as adj)	zimní	[zɪmni:]

month	měsíc (m)	[mnesi:ʦ]
this month	tento měsíc	[tɛnto mnesi:ʦ]
next month	příští měsíc	[prʃi:ʃti: mnesi:ʦ]
last month	minulý měsíc	[mɪnuli: mnesi:ʦ]

a month ago	před měsícem	[prʃɛd mnesi:ʦɛm]
in a month (a month later)	za měsíc	[za mnesi:ʦ]
in 2 months	za dva měsíce	[za dva mnesi:ʦɛ]
(2 months later)		
the whole month	celý měsíc	[ʦɛli: mnesi:ʦ]
all month long	celý měsíc	[ʦɛli: mnesi:ʦ]

monthly (~ magazine)	měsíční	[mnesi:ʧni:]
monthly (adv)	každý měsíc	[kaʒdi: mnesi:ʦ]
every month	měsíčně	[mnesi:ʧne]
twice a month	dvakrát měsíčně	[dvakra:t mnesi:ʧne]

year	rok (m)	[rok]
this year	letos	[lɛtos]
next year	příští rok	[prʃi:ʃti: rok]
last year	vloni	[vlonɪ]

a year ago	před rokem	[prʃɛd rokɛm]
in a year	za rok	[za rok]
in two years	za dva roky	[za dva rokɪ]
the whole year	celý rok	[ʦɛli: rok]
all year long	celý rok	[ʦɛli: rok]
every year	každý rok	[kaʒdi: rok]
annual (adj)	každoroční	[kaʒdorotʃni:]

| annually (adv) | každoročně | [kaʒdorotʃne] |
| 4 times a year | čtyřikrát za rok | [tʃtɪrʒɪkraːt za rok] |

date (e.g., today's ~)	datum (s)	[datum]
date (e.g., ~ of birth)	datum (s)	[datum]
calendar	kalendář (m)	[kalɛndaːrʃ]

half a year	půl roku	[puːl roku]
six months	půlrok (m)	[puːlrok]
season (summer, etc.)	období (s)	[obdobiː]
century	století (s)	[stolɛtiː]

TRAVEL. HOTEL

T&P Books Publishing

tourism, travel	turistika (ž)	[tʊrɪstɪka]
tourist	turista (m)	[tʊrɪsta]
trip, voyage	cestování (s)	[ʦɛstova:ni:]
adventure	příhoda (ž)	[prʃi:hoda]
trip, journey	cesta (ž)	[ʦɛsta]
vacation	dovolená (ž)	[dovolɛna:]
to be on vacation	mít dovolenou	[mi:t dovolɛnou]
rest	odpočinek (m)	[otpotʃɪnɛk]
train	vlak (m)	[vlak]
by train	vlakem	[vlakɛm]
airplane	letadlo (s)	[lɛtadlo]
by airplane	letadlem	[lɛtadlɛm]
by car	autem	[autɛm]
by ship	lodí	[lodi:]
luggage	zavazadla (s mn)	[zavazadla]
suitcase	kufr (m)	[kufr]
luggage cart	vozík (m) na zavazadla	[vozi:k na zavazadla]
passport	pas (m)	[pas]
visa	vízum (s)	[vi:zum]
ticket	jízdenka (ž)	[ji:zdɛŋka]
air ticket	letenka (ž)	[lɛtɛŋka]
guidebook	průvodce (m)	[pru:vodʦɛ]
map (tourist ~)	mapa (ž)	[mapa]
area (rural ~)	krajina (ž)	[krajɪna]
place, site	místo (s)	[mi:sto]
exotica (n)	exotika (ž)	[ɛgzotɪka]
exotic (adj)	exotický	[ɛgzotɪtʃki:]
amazing (adj)	podivuhodný	[podɪvuhodni:]
group	skupina (ž)	[skupɪna]
excursion, sightseeing tour	výlet (m)	[vi:lɛt]
guide (person)	průvodce (m)	[pru:vodʦɛ]

hotel	hotel (m)	[hotɛl]
motel	motel (m)	[motɛl]

three-star (~ hotel)	tři hvězdy	[trʃɪ hvezdɪ]
five-star	pět hvězd	[pet hvezt]
to stay (in a hotel, etc.)	ubytovat se	[ubɪtovat sɛ]

room	pokoj (m)	[pokoj]
single room	jednolůžkový pokoj (m)	[jɛdnolu:ʃkovi: pokoj]
double room	dvoulůžkový pokoj (m)	[dvoulu:ʃkovi: pokoj]
to book a room	rezervovat pokoj	[rɛzɛrvovat pokoj]

| half board | polopenze (ž) | [polopɛnzɛ] |
| full board | plná penze (ž) | [plna: pɛnzɛ] |

with bath	s koupelnou	[s koupɛlnou]
with shower	se sprchou	[sɛ sprxou]
satellite television	satelitní televize (ž)	[satɛlɪtni: tɛlɛvɪzɛ]
air-conditioner	klimatizátor (m)	[klɪmatɪza:tor]
towel	ručník (m)	[rutʃni:k]
key	klíč (m)	[kli:tʃ]

administrator	recepční (m)	[rɛtsɛptʃni:]
chambermaid	pokojská (ž)	[pokojska:]
porter, bellboy	nosič (m)	[nosɪtʃ]
doorman	vrátný (m)	[vra:tni:]

restaurant	restaurace (ž)	[rɛstauratsɛ]
pub, bar	bar (m)	[bar]
breakfast	snídaně (ž)	[sni:dane]
dinner	večeře (ž)	[vɛtʃɛrʒɛ]
buffet	obložený stůl (m)	[oblozeni: stu:l]

| lobby | vstupní hala (ž) | [vstupni: hala] |
| elevator | výtah (m) | [vi:tax] |

| DO NOT DISTURB | NERUŠIT | [nɛruʃɪt] |
| NO SMOKING | ZÁKAZ KOUŘENÍ | [za:kaz kourʒɛni:] |

22. Sightseeing

monument	památka (ž)	[pama:tka]
fortress	pevnost (ž)	[pɛvnost]
palace	palác (m)	[pala:ts]
castle	zámek (m)	[za:mɛk]
tower	věž (ž)	[vɛʃ]
mausoleum	mauzoleum (s)	[mauzolɛum]

architecture	architektura (ž)	[arxɪtɛktura]
medieval (adj)	středověký	[strʃɛdoveki:]
ancient (adj)	starobylý	[starobɪli:]
national (adj)	národní	[na:rodni:]
famous (monument, etc.)	známý	[zna:mi:]

tourist	**turista** (m)	[turɪsta]
guide (person)	**průvodce** (m)	[pru:vodʦɛ]
excursion, sightseeing tour	**výlet** (m)	[vi:lɛt]
to show (vt)	**ukazovat**	[ukazovat]
to tell (vt)	**povídat**	[povi:dat]
to find (vt)	**najít**	[naji:t]
to get lost (lose one's way)	**ztratit se**	[stratɪtsɛ]
map (e.g., subway ~)	**plán** (m)	[pla:n]
map (e.g., city ~)	**plán** (m)	[pla:n]
souvenir, gift	**suvenýr** (m)	[suvɛni:r]
gift shop	**prodejna** (ž) **suvenýrů**	[prodɛjna suvɛni:ru:]
to take pictures	**fotografovat**	[fotografovat]
to have one's picture taken	**fotografovat se**	[fotografovat sɛ]

TRANSPORTATION

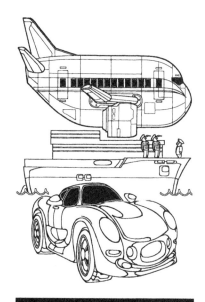

T&P Books Publishing

airport	letiště (s)	[lɛtɪʃte]
airplane	letadlo (s)	[lɛtadlo]
airline	letecká společnost (ž)	[lɛtɛtska: spolɛtʃnost]
air traffic controller	dispečer (m)	[dɪspɛtʃɛr]

departure	odlet (m)	[odlɛt]
arrival	přílet (m)	[prʃi:lɛt]
to arrive (by plane)	přiletět	[prʃɪlɛtet]

| departure time | čas (m) odletu | [tʃas odlɛtu] |
| arrival time | čas (m) příletu | [tʃas prʃilɛtu] |

| to be delayed | mít zpoždění | [mi:t spoʒdɛni:] |
| flight delay | zpoždění (s) odletu | [spoʒdeni: odlɛtu] |

information board	informační tabule (ž)	[ɪnformatʃni: tabulɛ]
information	informace (ž)	[ɪnformatsɛ]
to announce (vt)	hlásit	[hla:sɪt]
flight (e.g., next ~)	let (m)	[lɛt]

| customs | celnice (ž) | [tsɛlnɪtsɛ] |
| customs officer | celník (m) | [tsɛlni:k] |

customs declaration	prohlášení (s)	[prohla:ʃɛni:]
to fill out (vt)	vyplnit	[vɪplnɪt]
to fill out the declaration	vyplnit prohlášení	[vɪplnɪt prohla:ʃɛni:]
passport control	pasová kontrola (ž)	[pasova: kontrola]

luggage	zavazadla (s mn)	[zavazadla]
hand luggage	příruční zavazadlo (s)	[prʃi:rutʃni: zavazadlo]
luggage cart	vozík (m) na zavazadla	[vozi:k na zavazadla]

landing	přistání (s)	[prʃɪsta:ni:]
landing strip	přistávací dráha (ž)	[prʃɪsta:vatsi: dra:ha]
to land (vi)	přistávat	[prʃɪsta:vat]
airstair (passenger stair)	pojízdné schůdky (m mn)	[poji:zdnɛ: sxu:tkɪ]

check-in	registrace (ž)	[rɛgɪstratsɛ]
check-in counter	přepážka (ž) registrace	[prʃɛpa:ʃka rɛgɪstratsɛ]
to check-in (vi)	zaregistrovat se	[zarɛgɪstrovat sɛ]
boarding pass	palubní lístek (m)	[palubni: li:stɛk]
departure gate	příchod (m) k nástupu	[prʃi:xot k na:stupu]
transit	tranzit (m)	[tranzɪt]
to wait (vt)	čekat	[tʃɛkat]

departure lounge	čekárna (ž)	[tʃɛka:rna]
to see off	doprovázet	[doprova:zɛt]
to say goodbye	loučit se	[loutʃɪt sɛ]

24. Airplane

airplane	letadlo (s)	[lɛtadlo]
air ticket	letenka (ž)	[lɛtɛŋka]
airline	letecká společnost (ž)	[lɛtɛtska: spolɛtʃnost]
airport	letiště (s)	[lɛtɪʃtɛ]
supersonic (adj)	nadzvukový	[nadzvukovi:]

captain	velitel (m) posádky	[vɛlɪtɛl posa:tkɪ]
crew	posádka (ž)	[posa:tka]
pilot	pilot (m)	[pɪlot]
flight attendant (fem.)	letuška (ž)	[lɛtuʃka]
navigator	navigátor (m)	[navɪga:tor]

wings	křídla (s mn)	[krʃi:dla]
tail	ocas (m)	[oʦas]
cockpit	kabina (ž)	[kabɪna]
engine	motor (m)	[motor]
undercarriage (landing gear)	podvozek (m)	[podvozɛk]
turbine	turbína (ž)	[turbi:na]

propeller	vrtule (ž)	[vrtulɛ]
black box	černá skříňka (ž)	[tʃɛrna: skrʃi:nʲka]
yoke (control column)	řídicí páka (ž)	[rʒi:dɪtsi: pa:ka]
fuel	palivo (s)	[palɪvo]
safety card	předpis (m)	[prʃɛtpɪs]
oxygen mask	kyslíková maska (ž)	[kɪsli:kova: maska]
uniform	uniforma (ž)	[unɪforma]
life vest	záchranná vesta (ž)	[za:xranna: vɛsta]
parachute	padák (m)	[pada:k]

takeoff	start (m) letadla	[start lɛtadla]
to take off (vi)	vzlétat	[vzlɛ:tat]
runway	rozjezdová dráha (ž)	[rozjɛzdova: dra:ha]

visibility	viditelnost (ž)	[vɪdɪtɛlnost]
flight (act of flying)	let (m)	[lɛt]
altitude	výška (ž)	[vi:ʃka]
air pocket	vzdušná jáma (ž)	[vzduʃna: jama]

seat	místo (s)	[mi:sto]
headphones	sluchátka (s mn)	[sluxa:tka]
folding tray (tray table)	odklápěcí stolek (m)	[otkla:pɛtsi: stolɛk]
airplane window	okénko (s)	[okɛ:ŋko]
aisle	chodba (ž)	[xodba]

25. Train

train	vlak (m)	[vlak]
commuter train	elektrický vlak (m)	[ɛlɛktrɪtski: vlak]
express train	rychlík (m)	[rɪxli:k]
diesel locomotive	motorová lokomotiva (ž)	[motorova: lokomotɪva]
steam locomotive	parní lokomotiva (ž)	[parni: lokomotɪva]
passenger car	vůz (m)	[vu:z]
dining car	jídelní vůz (m)	[ji:dɛlni: vu:z]
rails	koleje (ž mn)	[kolɛjɛ]
railroad	železnice (ž mn)	[ʒelɛznɪtsɛ]
railway tie	pražec (m)	[praʒets]
platform (railway ~)	nástupiště (s)	[na:stupɪʃte]
track (~ 1, 2, etc.)	kolej (ž)	[kolɛj]
semaphore	návěstidlo (s)	[na:vestɪdlo]
station	stanice (ž)	[stanɪtsɛ]
engineer (train driver)	strojvůdce (m)	[strojvu:dtsɛ]
porter (of luggage)	nosič (m)	[nosɪtʃ]
car attendant	průvodčí (m)	[pru:vodtʃi:]
passenger	cestující (m)	[tsɛstuji:tsi:]
conductor (ticket inspector)	revizor (m)	[rɛvɪzor]
corridor (in train)	chodba (ž)	[xodba]
emergency brake	záchranná brzda (ž)	[za:xranna: brzda]
compartment	oddělení (s)	[oddelɛni:]
berth	lůžko (s)	[lu:ʃko]
upper berth	horní lůžko (s)	[horni: lu:ʃko]
lower berth	dolní lůžko (s)	[dolni: lu:ʃko]
bed linen, bedding	lůžkoviny (ž mn)	[lu:ʃkovɪnɪ]
ticket	jízdenka (ž)	[ji:zdɛŋka]
schedule	jízdní řád (m)	[ji:zdni: rʒa:t]
information display	tabule (ž)	[tabulɛ]
to leave, to depart	odjíždět	[odji:ʒdet]
departure (of train)	odjezd (m)	[odjɛst]
to arrive (ab. train)	přijíždět	[prʃɪji:ʒdet]
arrival	příjezd (m)	[prʃi:jɛst]
to arrive by train	přijet vlakem	[prʃɪɛt vlakɛm]
to get on the train	nastoupit do vlaku	[nastoupɪt do vlaku]
to get off the train	vystoupit z vlaku	[vɪstoupɪt z vlaku]
train wreck	železniční neštěstí (s)	[ʒelɛznɪtʃni: nɛʃtesti:]
to derail (vi)	vykolejit	[vɪkolɛjɪt]

steam locomotive	parní lokomotiva (ž)	[parni: lokomotɪva]
stoker, fireman	topič (m)	[topɪtʃ]
firebox	topeniště (s)	[topɛnɪʃte]
coal	uhlí (s)	[uhli:]

26. Ship

| ship | loď (ž) | [lotʲ] |
| vessel | loď (ž) | [lotʲ] |

steamship	parník (m)	[parni:k]
riverboat	říční loď (ž)	[ritʃni lotʲ]
cruise ship	linková loď (ž)	[lɪŋkova: lotʲ]
cruiser	křižník (m)	[krʒɪʒni:k]

yacht	jachta (ž)	[jaxta]
tugboat	vlek (m)	[vlɛk]
barge	vlečná nákladní loď (ž)	[vlɛtʃna: na:kladni: lotʲ]
ferry	prám (m)	[pra:m]

| sailing ship | plachetnice (ž) | [plaxɛtnɪtsɛ] |
| brigantine | brigantina (ž) | [brɪganti:na] |

| ice breaker | ledoborec (m) | [lɛdoborɛts] |
| submarine | ponorka (ž) | [ponorka] |

boat (flat-bottomed ~)	loďka (ž)	[loʲka]
dinghy	člun (m)	[tʃlun]
lifeboat	záchranný člun (m)	[za:xranni: tʃlun]
motorboat	motorový člun (m)	[motorovi: tʃlun]

captain	kapitán (m)	[kapɪta:n]
seaman	námořník (m)	[na:morʒni:k]
sailor	námořník (m)	[na:morʒni:k]
crew	posádka (ž)	[posa:tka]

boatswain	loďmistr (m)	[loʲmɪstr]
ship's boy	plavčík (m)	[plavtʃi:k]
cook	lodní kuchař (m)	[lodni: kuxarʃ]
ship's doctor	lodní lékař (m)	[lodni: lɛ:karʃ]

deck	paluba (ž)	[paluba]
mast	stěžeň (m)	[stɛʒenʲ]
sail	plachta (ž)	[plaxta]

hold	podpalubí (s)	[potpalubi:]
bow (prow)	příď (ž)	[prʃi:tʲ]
stern	záď (ž)	[za:tʲ]
oar	veslo (s)	[vɛslo]
screw propeller	lodní šroub (m)	[lodni: ʃroup]

cabin	kajuta (ž)	[kajuta]
wardroom	společenská místnost (ž)	[spolɛtʃɛnska: mi:stnost]
engine room	strojovna (ž)	[strojovna]
bridge	kapitánský můstek (m)	[kapɪta:nski: mu:stɛk]
radio room	rádiová kabina (ž)	[ra:dɪova: kabɪna]
wave (radio)	vlna (ž)	[vlna]
logbook	lodní deník (m)	[lodni: dɛni:k]

spyglass	dalekohled (m)	[dalɛkohlet]
bell	zvon (m)	[zvon]
flag	vlajka (ž)	[vlajka]

| hawser (mooring ~) | lano (s) | [lano] |
| knot (bowline, etc.) | uzel (m) | [uzɛl] |

| deckrails | zábradlí (s) | [za:bradli:] |
| gangway | schůdky (m mn) | [sxu:tkɪ] |

anchor	kotva (ž)	[kotva]
to weigh anchor	zvednout kotvy	[zvɛdnout kotvɪ]
to drop anchor	spustit kotvy	[spustɪt kotvɪ]
anchor chain	kotevní řetěz (m)	[kotɛvni: rʒɛtez]

port (harbor)	přístav (m)	[prʃi:staf]
quay, wharf	přístaviště (s)	[prʃi:stavɪʃte]
to berth (moor)	přistávat	[prʃɪsta:vat]
to cast off	vyplouvat	[vɪplouvat]

trip, voyage	cestování (s)	[tsɛstova:ni:]
cruise (sea trip)	výletní plavba (ž)	[vi:letni: plavba]
course (route)	kurz (m)	[kurs]
route (itinerary)	trasa (ž)	[trasa]

fairway (safe water channel)	plavební dráha (ž)	[plavɛbni: dra:ha]
shallows	mělčina (ž)	[mneltʃɪna]
to run aground	najet na mělčinu	[najɛt na mneltʃɪnu]

storm	bouřka (ž)	[bourʃka]
signal	signál (m)	[sɪgna:l]
to sink (vi)	potápět se	[pota:pet sɛ]
Man overboard!	Muž přes palubu!	[muʒ prʃɛs palubu]
SOS (distress signal)	SOS	[ɛs o: ɛs]
ring buoy	záchranný kruh (m)	[za:xranni: krux]

CITY

T&P Books Publishing

bus	autobus (m)	[autobus]
streetcar	tramvaj (ž)	[tramvaj]
trolley bus	trolejbus (m)	[trolɛjbus]
route (of bus, etc.)	trasa (ž)	[trasa]
number (e.g., bus ~)	číslo (s)	[tʃi:slo]

to go by ...	jet	[jɛt]
to get on (~ the bus)	nastoupit do ...	[nastoupɪt do]
to get off ...	vystoupit z ...	[vɪstoupɪt z]

stop (e.g., bus ~)	zastávka (ž)	[zasta:fka]
next stop	příští zastávka (ž)	[prʃi:ʃti: zasta:fka]
terminus	konečná stanice (ž)	[konɛtʃna: stanɪtsɛ]
schedule	jízdní řád (m)	[ji:zdni: rʒa:t]
to wait (vt)	čekat	[tʃɛkat]

| ticket | jízdenka (ž) | [ji:zdɛŋka] |
| fare | jízdné (s) | [ji:zdnɛ:] |

cashier (ticket seller)	pokladník (m)	[pokladni:k]
ticket inspection	kontrola (ž)	[kontrola]
ticket inspector	revizor (m)	[rɛvɪzor]

to be late (for ...)	mít zpoždění	[mi:t spoʒdɛni:]
to miss (~ the train, etc.)	opozdit se	[opozdɪt sɛ]
to be in a hurry	pospíchat	[pospi:xat]

taxi, cab	taxík (m)	[taksi:k]
taxi driver	taxikář (m)	[taksɪka:rʃ]
by taxi	taxíkem	[taksi:kɛm]
taxi stand	stanoviště (s) taxíků	[stanovɪʃte taksi:ku:]
to call a taxi	zavolat taxíka	[zavolat taksi:ka]
to take a taxi	vzít taxíka	[vzi:t taksi:ka]

traffic	uliční provoz (m)	[ulɪtʃni: provoz]
traffic jam	zácpa (ž)	[za:tspa]
rush hour	špička (ž)	[ʃpɪtʃka]
to park (vi)	parkovat se	[parkovat sɛ]
to park (vt)	parkovat	[parkovat]
parking lot	parkoviště (s)	[parkovɪʃte]

subway	metro (s)	[mɛtro]
station	stanice (ž)	[stanɪtsɛ]
to take the subway	jet metrem	[jɛt mɛtrɛm]

train	vlak (m)	[vlak]
train station	nádraží (s)	[na:draʒi:]

28. City. Life in the city

city, town	město (s)	[mnesto]
capital city	hlavní město (s)	[hlavni: mnesto]
village	venkov (m)	[vɛŋkof]

city map	plán (m) města	[pla:n mnesta]
downtown	střed (m) města	[strʃɛd mnesta]
suburb	předměstí (s)	[prʃɛdmnesti:]
suburban (adj)	předměstský	[prʃɛdmnestski:]

outskirts	okraj (m)	[okraj]
environs (suburbs)	okolí (s)	[okoli:]
city block	čtvrť (ž)	[tʃtvrtʲ]
residential block (area)	obytná čtvrť (ž)	[obɪtna: tʃtvrtʲ]

traffic	provoz (m)	[provoz]
traffic lights	semafor (m)	[sɛmafor]
public transportation	městská doprava (ž)	[mnestska: doprava]
intersection	křižovatka (ž)	[krʃɪʒovatka]

crosswalk	přechod (m)	[prʃɛxot]
pedestrian underpass	podchod (m)	[podxot]
to cross (~ the street)	přecházet	[prʃɛxa:zɛt]
pedestrian	chodec (m)	[xodɛts]
sidewalk	chodník (m)	[xodni:k]

bridge	most (m)	[most]
embankment (river walk)	nábřeží (s)	[na:brʒɛʒi:]
fountain	fontána (ž)	[fonta:na]

allée (garden walkway)	alej (ž)	[alɛj]
park	park (m)	[park]
boulevard	bulvár (m)	[bulva:r]
square	náměstí (s)	[na:mnesti:]
avenue (wide street)	třída (ž)	[trʃi:da]
street	ulice (ž)	[ulɪtsɛ]
side street	boční ulice (ž)	[botʃni: ulɪtsɛ]
dead end	slepá ulice (ž)	[slɛpa: ulɪtsɛ]

house	dům (m)	[du:m]
building	budova (ž)	[budova]
skyscraper	mrakodrap (m)	[mrakodrap]

facade	fasáda (ž)	[fasa:da]
roof	střecha (ž)	[strʃɛxa]
window	okno (s)	[okno]

arch	oblouk (m)	[oblouk]
column	sloup (m)	[sloup]
corner	roh (m)	[rox]

store window	výloha (ž)	[vi:loha]
signboard (store sign, etc.)	vývěsní tabule (ž)	[vi:vesni: tabulɛ]
poster (e.g., playbill)	plakát (m)	[plaka:t]
advertising poster	reklamní plakát (m)	[rɛklamni: plaka:t]
billboard	billboard (m)	[bɪlbo:rt]

garbage, trash	odpadky (m mn)	[otpatki:]
trash can (public ~)	popelnice (ž)	[popɛlnɪtsɛ]
to litter (vi)	dělat smetí	[delat smɛti:]
garbage dump	smetiště (s)	[smɛtɪʃte]

phone booth	telefonní budka (ž)	[tɛlɛfonni: butka]
lamppost	pouliční svítilna (ž)	[poulɪtʃni: svi:tɪlna]
bench (park ~)	lavička (ž)	[lavɪtʃka]

police officer	policista (m)	[polɪtsɪsta]
police	policie (ž)	[polɪtsɪe]
beggar	žebrák (m)	[ʒebra:k]
homeless (n)	bezdomovec (m)	[bɛzdomovɛts]

29. Urban institutions

store	obchod (m)	[obxot]
drugstore, pharmacy	lékárna (ž)	[lɛ:ka:rna]
eyeglass store	oční optika (ž)	[otʃni: optɪka]
shopping mall	obchodní středisko (s)	[obxodni: strʃɛdɪsko]
supermarket	supermarket (m)	[supɛrmarket]

bakery	pekařství (s)	[pɛkarʃstvi:]
baker	pekař (m)	[pɛkarʃ]
pastry shop	cukrárna (ž)	[tsukra:rna]
grocery store	smíšené zboží (s)	[smiʃɛnɛ: zboʒi:]
butcher shop	řeznictví (s)	[rʒɛznɪtstvi:]

| produce store | zelinářství (s) | [zɛlɪna:rʃstvi:] |
| market | tržnice (ž) | [trʒnɪtsɛ] |

coffee house	kavárna (ž)	[kava:rna]
restaurant	restaurace (ž)	[rɛstauratsɛ]
pub, bar	pivnice (ž)	[pɪvnɪtsɛ]
pizzeria	pizzerie (ž)	[pɪtsɛrɪe]

| hair salon | holičství (s) a kadeřnictví | [holɪtʃstvi: a kadɛrʒnɪtstvi:] |

| post office | pošta (ž) | [poʃta] |
| dry cleaners | čistírna (ž) | [tʃɪsti:rna] |

photo studio	fotografický ateliér (m)	[fotografɪtski: atɛlɪe:r]
shoe store	obchod (m) s obuví	[obxot s obuvi:]
bookstore	knihkupectví (s)	[knɪxkupɛtstvi:]
sporting goods store	sportovní potřeby (ž mn)	[sportovni: potrʃɛbɪ]

clothes repair shop	opravna (ž) oděvů	[opravna odevu:]
formal wear rental	půjčovna (ž) oděvů	[pu:jtʃovna odevu:]
video rental store	půjčovna (ž) filmů	[pu:jtʃovna fɪlmu:]

circus	cirkus (m)	[tsɪrkus]
zoo	zoologická zahrada (ž)	[zoologɪtska: zahrada]
movie theater	biograf (m)	[bɪograf]
museum	muzeum (s)	[muzɛum]
library	knihovna (ž)	[knɪhovna]

theater	divadlo (s)	[dɪvadlo]
opera (opera house)	opera (ž)	[opɛra]
nightclub	noční klub (m)	[notʃni: klup]
casino	kasino (s)	[kasi:no]

mosque	mešita (ž)	[mɛʃita]
synagogue	synagóga (ž)	[sinago:ga]
cathedral	katedrála (ž)	[katɛdra:la]
temple	chrám (m)	[xra:m]
church	kostel (m)	[kostɛl]

college	vysoká škola (ž)	[vɪsoka: ʃkola]
university	univerzita (ž)	[unɪvɛrzɪta]
school	škola (ž)	[ʃkola]

prefecture	prefektura (ž)	[prɛfɛktura]
city hall	magistrát (m)	[magɪstra:t]
hotel	hotel (m)	[hotɛl]
bank	banka (ž)	[baŋka]

embassy	velvyslanectví (s)	[vɛlvɪslanɛtstvi:]
travel agency	cestovní kancelář (ž)	[tsɛstovni: kantsɛla:rʃ]
information office	informační kancelář (ž)	[ɪnformatʃni: kantsɛla:rʃ]
currency exchange	směnárna (ž)	[smnena:rna]

| subway | metro (s) | [mɛtro] |
| hospital | nemocnice (ž) | [nɛmotsnɪtsɛ] |

| gas station | benzínová stanice (ž) | [bɛnzi:nova: stanɪtsɛ] |
| parking lot | parkoviště (s) | [parkovɪʃte] |

30. Signs

| signboard (store sign, etc.) | ukazatel (m) směru | [ukazatɛl smneru] |
| notice (door sign, etc.) | nápis (m) | [na:pɪs] |

poster	plakát (m)	[plaka:t]
direction sign	ukazatel (m)	[ukazatɛl]
arrow (sign)	šípka (ž)	[ʃi:pka]

caution	varování (s)	[varova:ni:]
warning sign	výstraha (ž)	[vi:straha]
to warn (vt)	upozorňovat	[upozornʲovat]

rest day (weekly ~)	volný den (m)	[volni: dɛn]
timetable (schedule)	jízdní řád (m)	[ji:zdni: rʒa:t]
opening hours	pracovní doba (ž)	[pratsovni: doba]

WELCOME!	VÍTEJTE!	[vi:tɛjtɛ]
ENTRANCE	VCHOD	[vxot]
EXIT	VÝCHOD	[vi:xot]

PUSH	TAM	[tam]
PULL	SEM	[sɛm]
OPEN	OTEVŘENO	[otɛvrʒɛno]
CLOSED	ZAVŘENO	[zavrʒɛno]

| WOMEN | ŽENY | [ʒenɪ] |
| MEN | MUŽI | [muʒɪ] |

| DISCOUNTS | SLEVY | [slɛvɪ] |
| SALE | VÝPRODEJ | [vi:prodɛj] |

| NEW! | NOVINKA! | [novɪŋka] |
| FREE | ZDARMA | [zdarma] |

ATTENTION!	POZOR!	[pozor]
NO VACANCIES	VOLNÁ MÍSTA NEJSOU	[volna: mi:sta nɛjsou]
RESERVED	ZADÁNO	[zada:no]

| ADMINISTRATION | KANCELÁŘ | [kantsɛla:rʒ] |
| STAFF ONLY | POUZE PRO PERSONÁL | [pouzɛ pro pɛrsona:l] |

BEWARE OF THE DOG!	POZOR! ZLÝ PES	[pozor zli: pɛs]
NO SMOKING	ZÁKAZ KOUŘENÍ	[za:kaz kourʒɛni:]
DO NOT TOUCH!	NEDOTÝKEJTE SE!	[nɛdoti:kɛjtɛ sɛ]

DANGEROUS	NEBEZPEČNÉ	[nɛbɛzpɛʧnɛ:]
DANGER	NEBEZPEČÍ	[nɛbɛzpɛʧi:]
HIGH VOLTAGE	VYSOKÉ NAPĚTÍ	[vɪsokɛ: napeti:]

| NO SWIMMING! | KOUPÁNÍ ZAKÁZÁNO | [koupa:ni: zaka:za:no] |
| OUT OF ORDER | MIMO PROVOZ | [mɪmo provoz] |

FLAMMABLE	VYSOCE HOŘLAVÝ	[vɪsotsɛ horʒlavi:]
FORBIDDEN	ZÁKAZ	[za:kaz]
NO TRESPASSING!	PRŮCHOD ZAKÁZÁN	[pru:xot zaka:za:n]
WET PAINT	ČERSTVĚ NATŘENO	[ʧɛrstvo natrʃɛno]

31. Shopping

to buy (purchase)	kupovat	[kupovat]
purchase	nákup (m)	[na:kup]
to go shopping	dělat nákupy	[delat na:kupɪ]
shopping	nakupování (s)	[nakupova:ni:]

| to be open (ab. store) | být otevřen | [bi:t otɛvrʒɛn] |
| to be closed | být zavřen | [bi:t zavrʒɛn] |

footwear, shoes	obuv (ž)	[obuf]
clothes, clothing	oblečení (s)	[oblɛtʃɛni:]
cosmetics	kosmetika (ž)	[kosmɛtɪka]
food products	potraviny (ž mn)	[potravɪnɪ]
gift, present	dárek (m)	[da:rɛk]

| salesman | prodavač (m) | [prodavatʃ] |
| saleswoman | prodavačka (ž) | [prodavatʃka] |

check out, cash desk	pokladna (ž)	[pokladna]
mirror	zrcadlo (s)	[zrtsadlo]
counter (store ~)	pult (m)	[pult]
fitting room	zkušební kabinka (ž)	[skuʃɛbni: kabɪŋka]

to try on	zkusit	[skusɪt]
to fit (ab. dress, etc.)	hodit se	[hodɪt sɛ]
to like (I like …)	líbit se	[li:bɪt sɛ]

price	cena (ž)	[tsɛna]
price tag	cenovka (ž)	[tsɛnofka]
to cost (vt)	stát	[sta:t]
How much?	Kolik?	[kolɪk]
discount	sleva (ž)	[slɛva]

inexpensive (adj)	levný	[lɛvni:]
cheap (adj)	levný	[lɛvni:]
expensive (adj)	drahý	[drahi:]
It's expensive	To je drahé	[to jɛ drahɛ:]

rental (n)	půjčování (s)	[pu:jtʃova:ni:]
to rent (~ a tuxedo)	vypůjčit si	[vɪpu:jtʃɪt sɪ]
credit (trade credit)	úvěr (m)	[u:ver]
on credit (adv)	na splátky	[na spla:tkɪ]

CLOTHING & ACCESSORIES

T&P Books Publishing

32. Outerwear. Coats

clothes	oblečení (s)	[oblɛtʃɛni:]
outerwear	svrchní oděv (m)	[svrxni: odef]
winter clothing	zimní oděv (m)	[zɪmni: odef]

coat (overcoat)	kabát (m)	[kaba:t]
fur coat	kožich (m)	[koʒɪx]
fur jacket	krátký kožich (m)	[kra:tki: koʒɪx]
down coat	peřová bunda (ž)	[pɛrʒova: bunda]

jacket (e.g., leather ~)	bunda (ž)	[bunda]
raincoat (trenchcoat, etc.)	plášť (m)	[pla:ʃtʲ]
waterproof (adj)	nepromokavý	[nɛpromokavi:]

33. Men's & women's clothing

shirt (button shirt)	košile (ž)	[koʃɪlɛ]
pants	kalhoty (ž mn)	[kalhotɪ]
jeans	džínsy (m mn)	[dʒi:nsɪ]
suit jacket	sako (s)	[sako]
suit	pánský oblek (m)	[pa:nski: oblɛk]

dress (frock)	šaty (m mn)	[ʃatɪ]
skirt	sukně (ž)	[suknɛ]
blouse	blůzka (ž)	[blu:ska]
knitted jacket (cardigan, etc.)	svetr (m)	[svɛtr]
jacket (of woman's suit)	žaket (m)	[ʒakɛt]

T-shirt	tričko (s)	[trɪtʃko]
shorts (short trousers)	šortky (ž mn)	[ʃortkɪ]
tracksuit	tepl’áková souprava (ž)	[tɛpla:kova: souprava]
bathrobe	župan (m)	[ʒupan]
pajamas	pyžamo (s)	[piʒamo]

| sweater | svetr (m) | [svɛtr] |
| pullover | pulovr (m) | [pulovr] |

vest	vesta (ž)	[vɛsta]
tailcoat	frak (m)	[frak]
tuxedo	smoking (m)	[smokɪŋk]
uniform	uniforma (ž)	[unɪforma]
workwear	pracovní oděv (m)	[pratsovni: odef]

| overalls | kombinéza (ž) | [kombɪnɛːza] |
| coat (e.g., doctor's smock) | plášť (m) | [plaːʃtʲ] |

34. Clothing. Underwear

underwear	spodní prádlo (s)	[spodni: praːdlo]
boxers, briefs	boxerky (mn)	[boksɛrkɪ]
panties	kalhotky (mn)	[kalhotkɪ]
undershirt (A-shirt)	tílko (s)	[tilko]
socks	ponožky (ž mn)	[ponoʃkɪ]

nightdress	noční košile (ž)	[notʃni: koʃɪlɛ]
bra	podprsenka (ž)	[potprsɛŋka]
knee highs	podkolenky (ž mn)	[potkolɛŋkɪ]
(knee-high socks)		
pantyhose	punčochové kalhoty (ž mn)	[puntʃoxovɛː kalgotɪ]
stockings (thigh highs)	punčochy (ž mn)	[puntʃoxɪ]
bathing suit	plavky (ž mn)	[plafkɪ]

35. Headwear

hat	čepice (ž)	[tʃɛpɪtsɛ]
fedora	klobouk (m)	[klobouk]
baseball cap	kšiltovka (ž)	[kʃɪltofka]
flatcap	čepice (ž)	[tʃɛpɪtsɛ]

beret	baret (m)	[barɛt]
hood	kapuce (ž)	[kaputsɛ]
panama hat	panamský klobouk (m)	[panamski: klobouk]
knit cap (knitted hat)	pletená čepice (ž)	[plɛtɛna: tʃɛpɪtsɛ]

| headscarf | šátek (m) | [ʃaːtɛk] |
| women's hat | kloboucek (m) | [kloboutʃɛk] |

hard hat	přilba (ž)	[prʃɪlba]
garrison cap	lodička (ž)	[lodɪtʃka]
helmet	helma (ž)	[hɛlma]

| derby | tvrďák (m) | [tvrdʲaːk] |
| top hat | válec (m) | [vaːlɛts] |

36. Footwear

footwear	obuv (ž)	[obuʃ]
shoes (men's shoes)	boty (ž mn)	[botɪ]
shoes (women's shoes)	střevíce (m mn)	[strʃɛviːtsɛ]

| boots (e.g., cowboy ~) | holínky (ž mn) | [holi:ŋkɪ] |
| slippers | bačkory (ž mn) | [batʃkorɪ] |

tennis shoes (e.g., Nike ~)	tenisky (ž mn)	[tɛnɪskɪ]
sneakers	kecky (ž mn)	[kɛtskɪ]
(e.g., Converse ~)		
sandals	sandály (m mn)	[sanda:lɪ]

cobbler (shoe repairer)	obuvník (m)	[obuvni:k]
heel	podpatek (m)	[potpatɛk]
pair (of shoes)	pár (m)	[pa:r]

| shoestring | tkanička (ž) | [tkanɪtʃka] |
| to lace (vt) | šněrovat | [ʃnerovat] |

| shoehorn | lžíce (ž) na boty | [ʒi:tsɛ na botɪ] |
| shoe polish | krém (m) na boty | [krɛ:m na botɪ] |

37. Personal accessories

gloves	rukavice (ž mn)	[rukavɪtsɛ]
mittens	palčáky (m mn)	[paltʃa:kɪ]
scarf (muffler)	šála (ž)	[ʃa:la]

glasses (eyeglasses)	brýle (ž mn)	[bri:lɛ]
frame (eyeglass ~)	obroučky (m mn)	[obroutʃkɪ]
umbrella	deštník (m)	[dɛʃtni:k]
walking stick	hůl (ž)	[hu:l]

| hairbrush | kartáč (m) na vlasy | [karta:tʃ na vlasɪ] |
| fan | vějíř (m) | [veji:rʃ] |

| tie (necktie) | kravata (ž) | [kravata] |
| bow tie | motýlek (m) | [moti:lɛk] |

| suspenders | šle (ž mn) | [ʃlɛ] |
| handkerchief | kapesník (m) | [kapesni:k] |

| comb | hřeben (m) | [hrʒɛbɛn] |
| barrette | sponka (ž) | [spoŋka] |

| hairpin | vlásnička (ž) | [vla:snɪtʃka] |
| buckle | spona (ž) | [spona] |

| belt | pás (m) | [pa:s] |
| shoulder strap | řemen (m) | [rʒɛmɛn] |

bag (handbag)	taška (ž)	[taʃka]
purse	kabelka (ž)	[kabɛlka]
backpack	batoh (m)	[batox]

38. Clothing. Miscellaneous

fashion	móda (ž)	[mo:da]
in vogue (adj)	módní	[mo:dni:]
fashion designer	modelář (m)	[modɛla:rʃ]

collar	límec (m)	[li:mɛʦ]
pocket	kapsa (ž)	[kapsa]
pocket (as adj)	kapesní	[kapɛsni:]
sleeve	rukáv (m)	[ruka:f]
hanging loop	poutko (s)	[poutko]
fly (on trousers)	poklopec (m)	[poklopɛʦ]

zipper (fastener)	zip (m)	[zɪp]
fastener	spona (ž)	[spona]
button	knoflík (m)	[knofli:k]
buttonhole	knoflíková dírka (ž)	[knofli:kova: di:rka]
to come off (ab. button)	utrhnout se	[utrhnout sɛ]

to sew (vi, vt)	šít	[ʃi:t]
to embroider (vi, vt)	vyšívat	[vɪʃi:vat]
embroidery	výšivka (ž)	[vi:ʃɪfka]
sewing needle	jehla (ž)	[jɛhla]
thread	nit (ž)	[nɪt]
seam	šev (m)	[ʃɛf]

to get dirty (vi)	ušpinit se	[uʃpɪnɪt sɛ]
stain (mark, spot)	skvrna (ž)	[skvrna]
to crease, crumple (vi)	pomačkat se	[pomaʧkat sɛ]
to tear, to rip (vt)	roztrhat	[roztrhat]
clothes moth	mol (m)	[mol]

39. Personal care. Cosmetics

toothpaste	zubní pasta (ž)	[zubni: pasta]
toothbrush	kartáček (m) na zuby	[karta:ʧɛk na zubɪ]
to brush one's teeth	čistit si zuby	[ʧɪstɪt sɪ zubɪ]

razor	holicí strojek (m)	[holɪʦi: strojɛk]
shaving cream	krém (m) na holení	[krɛ:m na holɛni:]
to shave (vi)	holit se	[holɪt sɛ]

| soap | mýdlo (s) | [mi:dlo] |
| shampoo | šampon (m) | [ʃampon] |

scissors	nůžky (ž mn)	[nu:ʃkɪ]
nail file	pilník (m) na nehty	[pɪlni:k na nɛxtɪ]
nail clippers	kleštičky (ž mn) na nehty	[klɛʃtɪʧkɪ na nɛxtɪ]
tweezers	pinzeta (ž)	[pɪnzeta]

cosmetics	kosmetika (ž)	[kosmɛtɪka]
face mask	kosmetická maska (ž)	[kosmɛtɪtska: maska]
manicure	manikúra (ž)	[manɪku:ra]
to have a manicure	dělat manikúru	[delat manɪku:ru]
pedicure	pedikúra (ž)	[pɛdɪku:ra]

make-up bag	kosmetická kabelka (ž)	[kosmɛtɪtska: kabɛlka]
face powder	pudr (m)	[pudr]
powder compact	pudřenka (ž)	[pudrʒɛŋka]
blusher	červené líčidlo (s)	[tʃɛrvɛnɛ: li:tʃɪdlo]

perfume (bottled)	voňavka (ž)	[vonʲafka]
toilet water (lotion)	toaletní voda (ž)	[toalɛtni: voda]
lotion	pleťová voda (ž)	[plɛtʲova: voda]
cologne	kolínská voda (ž)	[koli:nska: voda]

eyeshadow	oční stíny (m mn)	[otʃni: sti:nɪ]
eyeliner	tužka (ž) na oči	[tuʃka na otʃɪ]
mascara	řasenka (ž)	[rʒasɛŋka]

lipstick	rtěnka (ž)	[rteŋka]
nail polish, enamel	lak (m) na nehty	[lak na nɛxtɪ]
hair spray	lak (m) na vlasy	[lak na vlasɪ]
deodorant	deodorant (m)	[dɛodorant]

cream	krém (m)	[krɛ:m]
face cream	pleťový krém (m)	[plɛtʲovi: krɛ:m]
hand cream	krém (m) na ruce	[krɛ:m na rutsɛ]
anti-wrinkle cream	krém (m) proti vráskám	[krɛ:m protɪ vra:ska:m]
day cream	denní krém (m)	[dɛnni:]krɛ:m]
night cream	noční krém (m)	[notʃni: krɛ:m]
day (as adj)	denní	[dɛnni:]
night (as adj)	noční	[notʃni:]

tampon	tampón (m)	[tampo:n]
toilet paper (toilet roll)	toaletní papír (m)	[toalɛtni: papi:r]
hair dryer	fén (m)	[fɛ:n]

40. Watches. Clocks

watch (wristwatch)	hodinky (ž mn)	[hodɪŋkɪ]
dial	ciferník (m)	[tsɪfɛrni:k]
hand (of clock, watch)	ručička (ž)	[rutʃɪtʃka]
metal watch band	náramek (m)	[na:ramɛk]
watch strap	pásek (m)	[pa:sɛk]

battery	baterka (ž)	[batɛrka]
to be dead (battery)	vybít se	[vɪbi:t sɛ]
to change a battery	vyměnit baterku	[vɪmnɛnɪt batɛrku]
to run fast	jít napřed	[ji:t naprʃɛt]

to run slow	opožďovat se	[opoʒdʲovat sɛ]
wall clock	nástěnné hodiny (ž mn)	[naːstennɛː hodɪnɪ]
hourglass	přesýpací hodiny (ž mn)	[prʃɛsiːpatsi: hodɪnɪ]
sundial	sluneční hodiny (ž mn)	[slunɛtʃni: hodɪnɪ]
alarm clock	budík (m)	[budiːk]
watchmaker	hodinář (m)	[hodɪnaːrʃ]
to repair (vt)	opravovat	[opravovat]

EVERYDAY EXPERIENCE

T&P Books Publishing

money	peníze (m mn)	[pɛni:zɛ]
currency exchange	výměna (ž)	[vi:mnena]
exchange rate	kurz (m)	[kurs]
ATM	bankomat (m)	[baŋkomat]
coin	mince (ž)	[mɪntsɛ]

| dollar | dolar (m) | [dolar] |
| euro | euro (s) | [ɛuro] |

lira	lira (ž)	[lɪra]
Deutschmark	marka (ž)	[marka]
franc	frank (m)	[fraŋk]
pound sterling	libra (ž) šterlinků	[lɪbra ʃtɛrlɪŋku:]
yen	jen (m)	[jɛn]

debt	dluh (m)	[dlux]
debtor	dlužník (m)	[dluʒni:k]
to lend (money)	půjčit	[pu:jtʃɪt]
to borrow (vi, vt)	půjčit si	[pu:jtʃɪt sɪ]

bank	banka (ž)	[baŋka]
account	účet (m)	[u:tʃɛt]
to deposit (vt)	uložit	[uloʒɪt]
to deposit into the account	uložit na účet	[uloʒɪt na u:tʃɛt]
to withdraw (vt)	vybrat z účtu	[vɪbrat s u:tʃtu]

credit card	kreditní karta (ž)	[krɛdɪtni: karta]
cash	hotové peníze (m mn)	[hotovɛ: pɛni:zɛ]
check	šek (m)	[ʃɛk]
to write a check	vystavit šek	[vɪstavɪt ʃɛk]
checkbook	šeková knížka (ž)	[ʃɛkova: kni:ʃka]

wallet	náprsní taška (ž)	[na:prsni: taʃka]
change purse	peněženka (ž)	[pɛneʒeŋka]
safe	trezor (m)	[trɛzor]

heir	dědic (m)	[dedɪts]
inheritance	dědictví (s)	[dedɪtstvi:]
fortune (wealth)	majetek (m)	[majɛtɛk]

lease	nájem (m)	[na:jɛm]
rent (money)	činže (ž)	[tʃɪnʒe]
to rent (sth from sb)	pronajímat si	[pronaji:mat sɪ]
price	cena (ž)	[tsɛna]

| cost | cena (ž) | [tsɛna] |
| sum | částka (ž) | [tʃa:stka] |

to spend (vt)	utrácet	[utra:tsɛt]
expenses	náklady (m mn)	[na:kladɪ]
to economize (vi, vt)	šetřit	[ʃɛtrʃɪt]
economical	úsporný	[u:sporni:]

to pay (vi, vt)	platit	[platɪt]
payment	platba (ž)	[platba]
change (give the ~)	peníze (m mn) nazpět	[pɛni:zɛ naspet]

tax	daň (ž)	[danʲ]
fine	pokuta (ž)	[pokuta]
to fine (vt)	pokutovat	[pokutovat]

42. Post. Postal service

post office	pošta (ž)	[poʃta]
mail (letters, etc.)	pošta (ž)	[poʃta]
mailman	listonoš (m)	[lɪstonoʃ]
opening hours	pracovní doba (ž)	[pratsovni: doba]

letter	dopis (m)	[dopɪs]
registered letter	doporučený dopis (m)	[doporutʃɛni: dopɪs]
postcard	pohlednice (ž)	[pohlɛdnɪtsɛ]
telegram	telegram (m)	[tɛlɛgram]
package (parcel)	balík (m)	[bali:k]
money transfer	peněžní poukázka (ž)	[pɛneʒni: pouka:ska]

to receive (vt)	dostat	[dostat]
to send (vt)	odeslat	[odɛslat]
sending	odeslání (s)	[odɛsla:ni:]

address	adresa (ž)	[adrɛsa]
ZIP code	poštovní směrovací číslo (s)	[poʃtovni: smnerovatsi: tʃi:slo]
sender	odesílatel (m)	[odɛsi:latɛl]
receiver	příjemce (m)	[prʃi:jɛmtsɛ]

| name (first name) | jméno (s) | [jmɛ:no] |
| surname (last name) | příjmení (s) | [prʃi:jmɛni:] |

postage rate	tarif (m)	[tarɪf]
standard (adj)	obyčejný	[obɪtʃɛjni:]
economical (adj)	zlevněný	[zlɛvneni:]

weight	váha (ž)	[va:ha]
to weigh (~ letters)	vážit	[va:ʒɪt]
envelope	obálka (ž)	[oba:lka]

| postage stamp | známka (ž) | [zna:mka] |
| to stamp an envelope | nalepovat známku | [nalɛpovat zna:mku] |

43. Banking

| bank | banka (ž) | [baŋka] |
| branch (of bank, etc.) | pobočka (ž) | [pobotʃka] |

| bank clerk, consultant | konzultant (m) | [konzultant] |
| manager (director) | správce (m) | [spra:vtsɛ] |

| bank account | účet (m) | [u:tʃɛt] |
| account number | číslo (s) účtu | [tʃi:slo u:tʃtu] |

| checking account | běžný účet (m) | [beʒni: u:tʃɛt] |
| savings account | spořitelní účet (m) | [sporʒitɛlni: u:tʃɛt] |

| to open an account | založit účet | [zaloʒit u:tʃɛt] |
| to close the account | uzavřít účet | [uzavrʒi:t u:tʃɛt] |

| to deposit into the account | uložit na účet | [uloʒit na u:tʃɛt] |
| to withdraw (vt) | vybrat z účtu | [vɪbrat s u:tʃtu] |

| deposit | vklad (m) | [fklat] |
| to make a deposit | uložit vklad | [uloʒɪt fklat] |

| wire transfer | převod (m) | [prʃɛvot] |
| to wire, to transfer | převést | [prʃɛvɛ:st] |

| sum | částka (ž) | [tʃa:stka] |
| How much? | Kolik? | [kolɪk] |

| signature | podpis (m) | [potpɪs] |
| to sign (vt) | podepsat | [podɛpsat] |

| credit card | kreditní karta (ž) | [krɛdɪtni: karta] |
| code (PIN code) | kód (m) | [ko:t] |

| credit card number | číslo (s) kreditní karty | [tʃi:slo krɛdɪtni: kartɪ] |
| ATM | bankomat (m) | [baŋkomat] |

check	šek (m)	[ʃɛk]
to write a check	vystavit šek	[vɪstavɪt ʃɛk]
checkbook	šeková knížka (ž)	[ʃɛkova: kni:ʃka]

loan (bank ~)	úvěr (m)	[u:ver]
to apply for a loan	žádat o úvěr	[ʒa:dat o u:ver]
to get a loan	brát na úvěr	[bra:t na u:ver]
to give a loan	poskytovat úvěr	[poskɪtovat u:ver]
guarantee	kauce (ž)	[kautsɛ]

44. Telephone. Phone conversation

telephone	telefon (m)	[tɛlɛfon]
cell phone	mobilní telefon (m)	[mobɪlni: tɛlɛfon]
answering machine	záznamník (m)	[za:znamni:k]

| to call (by phone) | volat | [volat] |
| phone call | hovor (m), volání (s) | [hovor], [vola:ni:] |

to dial a number	vytočit číslo	[vɪtotʃɪt tʃi:slo]
Hello!	Prosím!	[prosi:m]
to ask (vt)	zeptat se	[zɛptat sɛ]
to answer (vi, vt)	odpovědět	[otpovedet]

to hear (vt)	slyšet	[slɪʃɛt]
well (adv)	dobře	[dobrʒɛ]
not well (adv)	špatně	[ʃpatne]
noises (interference)	poruchy (ž mn)	[poruxɪ]

receiver	sluchátko (s)	[sluxa:tko]
to pick up (~ the phone)	vzít sluchátko	[vzi:t sluxa:tko]
to hang up (~ the phone)	zavěsit sluchátko	[zavesɪt sluxa:tko]

busy (engaged)	obsazeno	[opsazɛno]
to ring (ab. phone)	zvonit	[zvonɪt]
telephone book	telefonní seznam (m)	[tɛlɛfonni: sɛznam]

local (adj)	místní	[mi:stni:]
local call	místní hovor (m)	[mi:stni: hovor]
long distance (~ call)	dálkový	[da:lkovi:]
long-distance call	dálkový hovor (m)	[da:lkovi: hovor]
international (adj)	mezinárodní	[mɛzɪna:rodni:]
international call	mezinárodní hovor (m)	[mɛzɪna:rodni: hovor]

45. Cell phone

cell phone	mobilní telefon (m)	[mobɪlni: tɛlɛfon]
display	displej (m)	[dɪsplɛj]
button	tlačítko (s)	[tlatʃi:tko]
SIM card	SIM karta (ž)	[sɪm karta]

battery	baterie (ž)	[batɛrɪe]
to be dead (battery)	vybít se	[vɪbi:t sɛ]
charger	nabíječka (ž)	[nabi:jɛtʃka]

menu	nabídka (ž)	[nabi:tka]
settings	nastavení (s)	[nastavɛni:]
tune (melody)	melodie (ž)	[mɛlodɪe]
to select (vt)	vybrat	[vɪbrat]

calculator	kalkulačka (ž)	[kalkulaʧka]
voice mail	hlasová schránka (ž)	[hlasova: sxra:ŋka]
alarm clock	budík (m)	[budi:k]
contacts	telefonní seznam (m)	[tɛlɛfonni: sɛznam]

| SMS (text message) | SMS zpráva (ž) | [ɛsɛmɛs spra:va] |
| subscriber | účastník (m) | [u:ʧastni:k] |

46. Stationery

| ballpoint pen | pero (s) | [pɛro] |
| fountain pen | plnicí pero (s) | [plnɪʦi: pɛro] |

pencil	tužka (ž)	[tuʃka]
highlighter	značkovač (m)	[znaʧkovaʧ]
felt-tip pen	fix (m)	[fɪks]

| notepad | notes (m) | [notɛs] |
| agenda (diary) | diář (m) | [dɪa:rʃ] |

ruler	pravítko (s)	[pravi:tko]
calculator	kalkulačka (ž)	[kalkulaʧka]
eraser	guma (ž)	[guma]
thumbtack	napínáček (m)	[napi:na:ʧɛk]
paper clip	svorka (ž)	[svorka]

glue	lepidlo (s)	[lɛpɪdlo]
stapler	sešívačka (ž)	[sɛʃi:vaʧka]
hole punch	dírkovačka (ž)	[di:rkovaʧka]
pencil sharpener	ořezávátko (s)	[orʒɛza:va:tko]

47. Foreign languages

language	jazyk (m)	[jazɪk]
foreign (adj)	cizí	[ʦɪzi:]
foreign language	cizí jazyk (m)	[ʦɪzi: jazɪk]
to study (vt)	studovat	[studovat]
to learn (language, etc.)	učit se	[uʧɪt sɛ]

to read (vi, vt)	číst	[ʧi:st]
to speak (vi, vt)	mluvit	[mluvɪt]
to understand (vt)	rozumět	[rozumet]
to write (vt)	psát	[psa:t]

fast (adv)	rychle	[rɪxlɛ]
slowly (adv)	pomalu	[pomalu]
fluently (adv)	plynně	[plɪnnə]
rules	pravidla (s mn)	[pravɪdla]

grammar	mluvnice (ž)	[mluvnɪtsɛ]
vocabulary	slovní zásoba (ž)	[slovni: za:soba]
phonetics	hláskosloví (s)	[hla:skoslovi:]

textbook	učebnice (ž)	[utʃɛbnɪtsɛ]
dictionary	slovník (m)	[slovni:k]
teach-yourself book	učebnice (ž) pro samouky	[utʃɛbnɪtsɛ pro samoukɪ]
phrasebook	konverzace (ž)	[konvɛrzatsɛ]

cassette, tape	kazeta (ž)	[kazɛta]
videotape	videokazeta (ž)	[vɪdɛokazɛta]
CD, compact disc	CD disk (m)	[tsɛ:dɛ: dɪsk]
DVD	DVD (s)	[dɛvɛdɛ]

alphabet	abeceda (ž)	[abɛtsɛda]
to spell (vt)	hláskovat	[hla:skovat]
pronunciation	výslovnost (ž)	[vi:slovnost]

accent	cizí přízvuk (m)	[tsɪzi: prʃi:zvuk]
with an accent	s cizím přízvukem	[s tsɪzi:m prʃi:zvukɛm]
without an accent	bez cizího přízvuku	[bɛz tsɪzi:ho prʃi:zvuku]

| word | slovo (s) | [slovo] |
| meaning | smysl (m) | [smɪsl] |

course (e.g., a French ~)	kurzy (m mn)	[kurzɪ]
to sign up	zapsat se	[zapsat sɛ]
teacher	vyučující (m)	[vɪutʃuji:tsi:]

translation (process)	překlad (m)	[prʃɛklat]
translation (text, etc.)	překlad (m)	[prʃɛklat]
translator	překladatel (m)	[prʃɛkladatɛl]
interpreter	tlumočník (m)	[tlumotʃni:k]

| polyglot | polyglot (m) | [polɪglot] |
| memory | paměť (ž) | [pamnetʲ] |

MEALS. RESTAURANT

T&P Books Publishing

48. Table setting

spoon	lžíce (ž)	[ʒiːtsɛ]
knife	nůž (m)	[nuːʃ]
fork	vidlička (ž)	[vɪdlɪtʃka]

cup (e.g., coffee ~)	šálek (m)	[ʃaːlɛk]
plate (dinner ~)	talíř (m)	[taliːrʃ]
saucer	talířek (m)	[taliːrʒɛk]
napkin (on table)	ubrousek (m)	[ubrousɛk]
toothpick	párátko (s)	[paːraːtko]

49. Restaurant

restaurant	restaurace (ž)	[rɛstauratsɛ]
coffee house	kavárna (ž)	[kavaːrna]
pub, bar	bar (m)	[bar]
tearoom	čajovna (ž)	[tʃajovna]

waiter	číšník (m)	[tʃiːʃniːk]
waitress	číšnice (ž)	[tʃiːʃnɪtsɛ]
bartender	barman (m)	[barman]
menu	jídelní lístek (m)	[jiːdɛlni: liːstɛk]
wine list	nápojový lístek (m)	[naːpojovi: liːstɛk]
to book a table	rezervovat stůl	[rɛzɛrvovat stuːl]
course, dish	jídlo (s)	[jiːdlo]
to order (meal)	objednat si	[objɛdnat sɪ]
to make an order	objednat si	[objɛdnat sɪ]

aperitif	aperitiv (m)	[apɛrɪtɪʃ]
appetizer	předkrm (m)	[prʃɛtkrm]
dessert	desert (m)	[dɛsɛrt]

check	účet (m)	[uːtʃɛt]
to pay the check	zaplatit účet	[zaplatɪt uːtʃɛt]
to give change	dát nazpátek	[daːt naspaːtɛk]
tip	spropitné (s)	[spropɪtnɛː]

50. Meals

food	jídlo (s)	[jiːdlʊ]
to eat (vi, vt)	jíst	[jiːst]

breakfast	snídaně (ž)	[sni:dane]
to have breakfast	snídat	[sni:dat]
lunch	oběd (m)	[obet]
to have lunch	obědvat	[obedvat]
dinner	večeře (ž)	[vɛtʃɛrʒɛ]
to have dinner	večeřet	[vɛtʃɛrʒɛt]

| appetite | chuť (ž) k jídlu | [xutʲ k ji:dlu] |
| Enjoy your meal! | Dobrou chuť! | [dobrou xutʲ] |

to open (~ a bottle)	otvírat	[otvi:rat]
to spill (liquid)	rozlít	[rozli:t]
to spill out (vi)	rozlít se	[rozli:t sɛ]

to boil (vi)	vřít	[vrʒi:t]
to boil (vt)	vařit	[varʒɪt]
boiled (~ water)	svařený	[svarʒɛni:]
to chill, cool down (vt)	ochladit	[oxladɪt]
to chill (vi)	ochlazovat se	[oxlazovat sɛ]

| taste, flavor | chuť (ž) | [xutʲ] |
| aftertaste | příchuť (ž) | [prʃi:xutʲ] |

to slim down (lose weight)	držet dietu	[drʒet dɪetu]
diet	dieta (ž)	[dɪeta]
vitamin	vitamín (m)	[vɪtami:n]
calorie	kalorie (ž)	[kalorɪe]
vegetarian (n)	vegetarián (m)	[vɛgɛtarɪa:n]
vegetarian (adj)	vegetariánský	[vɛgɛtarɪa:nski:]

fats (nutrient)	tuky (m)	[tukɪ]
proteins	bílkoviny (ž)	[bi:lkovɪnɪ]
carbohydrates	karbohydráty (mn)	[karbohɪdrati:]
slice (of lemon, ham)	plátek (m)	[pla:tɛk]
piece (of cake, pie)	kousek (m)	[kousɛk]
crumb	drobek (m)	[drobɛk]
(of bread, cake, etc.)		

51. Cooked dishes

course, dish	jídlo (s)	[ji:dlo]
cuisine	kuchyně (ž)	[kuxɪne]
recipe	recept (m)	[rɛtsɛpt]
portion	porce (ž)	[portsɛ]

| salad | salát (m) | [sala:t] |
| soup | polévka (ž) | [polɛ:fka] |

| clear soup (broth) | vývar (m) | [vi:var] |
| sandwich (bread) | obložený chlebíček (m) | [oblɔʒeni: xlɛbi:tʃɛk] |

fried eggs	míchaná vejce (s mn)	[mi:xana: vɛjtsɛ]
hamburger (beefburger)	hamburger (m)	[hamburgɛr]
beefsteak	biftek (m)	[bɪftɛk]

side dish	příloha (ž)	[prʃi:loha]
spaghetti	spagety (m mn)	[spagɛtɪ]
mashed potatoes	bramborová kaše (ž)	[bramborova: kaʃɛ]
pizza	pizza (ž)	[pɪtsa]
porridge (oatmeal, etc.)	kaše (ž)	[kaʃɛ]
omelet	omeleta (ž)	[omɛlɛta]

boiled (e.g., ~ beef)	vařený	[varʒɛni:]
smoked (adj)	uzený	[uzɛni:]
fried (adj)	smažený	[smaʒeni:]
dried (adj)	sušený	[suʃɛni:]
frozen (adj)	zmražený	[zmraʒeni:]
pickled (adj)	marinovaný	[marɪnovani:]

sweet (sugary)	sladký	[slatki:]
salty (adj)	slaný	[slani:]
cold (adj)	studený	[studɛni:]
hot (adj)	teplý	[tɛpli:]
bitter (adj)	hořký	[horʃki:]
tasty (adj)	chutný	[xutni:]

to cook in boiling water	vařit	[varʒɪt]
to cook (dinner)	vařit	[varʒɪt]
to fry (vt)	smažit	[smaʒɪt]
to heat up (food)	ohřívat	[ohrʒi:vat]

to salt (vt)	solit	[solɪt]
to pepper (vt)	pepřit	[pɛprʃɪt]
to grate (vt)	strouhat	[strouhat]
peel (n)	slupka (ž)	[slupka]
to peel (vt)	loupat	[loupat]

52. Food

meat	maso (s)	[maso]
chicken	slepice (ž)	[slɛpɪtsɛ]
Rock Cornish hen (poussin)	kuře (s)	[kurʒɛ]
duck	kachna (ž)	[kaxna]
goose	husa (ž)	[husa]
game	zvěřina (ž)	[zverʒɪna]
turkey	krůta (ž)	[kru:ta]

pork	vepřové (s)	[vɛprʃovɛ:]
veal	telecí (s)	[tɛlɛtsi:]
lamb	skopové (s)	[skopovɛ:]

| beef | hovězí (s) | [hovezi:] |
| rabbit | králík (m) | [kra:li:k] |

| sausage (bologna, etc.) | salám (m) | [sala:m] |
| vienna sausage (frankfurter) | párek (m) | [pa:rɛk] |

bacon	slanina (ž)	[slanɪna]
ham	šunka (ž)	[ʃuŋka]
gammon	kýta (ž)	[ki:ta]

pâté	paštika (ž)	[paʃtɪka]
liver	játra (s mn)	[ja:tra]
hamburger (ground beef)	mleté maso (s)	[mlɛtɛ: maso]
tongue	jazyk (m)	[jazɪk]

egg	vejce (s)	[vɛjtsɛ]
eggs	vejce (s mn)	[vɛjtsɛ]
egg white	bílek (m)	[bi:lɛk]
egg yolk	žloutek (m)	[ʒloutɛk]

fish	ryby (ž mn)	[rɪbɪ]
seafood	mořské plody (m mn)	[morʃkɛ: plodɪ]
crustaceans	korýši (m mn)	[kori:ʃɪ]
caviar	kaviár (m)	[kavɪa:r]

crab	krab (m)	[krap]
shrimp	kreveta (ž)	[krɛvɛta]
oyster	ústřice (ž)	[u:strʃɪtsɛ]
spiny lobster	langusta (ž)	[langusta]
octopus	chobotnice (ž)	[xobotnɪtsɛ]
squid	sépie (ž)	[sɛ:pɪe]

sturgeon	jeseter (m)	[jɛsɛtɛr]
salmon	losos (m)	[losos]
halibut	platýs (m)	[plati:s]

cod	treska (ž)	[trɛska]
mackerel	makrela (ž)	[makrɛla]
tuna	tuňák (m)	[tunʲa:k]
eel	úhoř (m)	[u:horʃ]

trout	pstruh (m)	[pstrux]
sardine	sardinka (ž)	[sardɪŋka]
pike	štika (ž)	[ʃtɪka]
herring	sleď (ž)	[slɛtʲ]

bread	chléb (m)	[xlɛ:p]
cheese	sýr (m)	[si:r]
sugar	cukr (m)	[tsukr]
salt	sůl (ž)	[su:l]
rice	rýže (ž)	[ri:ʒe]
pasta (macaroni)	makaróny (m mn)	[makaro:nɪ]

noodles	nudle (ž mn)	[nudlɛ]
butter	máslo (s)	[ma:slo]
vegetable oil	olej (m)	[olɛj]
sunflower oil	slunečnicový olej (m)	[slunɛtʃnɪtsovi: olɛj]
margarine	margarín (m)	[margari:n]

| olives | olivy (ž) | [olɪvɪ] |
| olive oil | olivový olej (m) | [olɪvovi: olɛj] |

milk	mléko (s)	[mlɛ:ko]
condensed milk	kondenzované mléko (s)	[kondɛnzovanɛ: mlɛ:ko]
yogurt	jogurt (m)	[jogurt]
sour cream	kyselá smetana (ž)	[kɪsɛla: smɛtana]
cream (of milk)	sladká smetana (ž)	[slatka: smɛtana]

| mayonnaise | majonéza (ž) | [majonɛ:za] |
| buttercream | krém (m) | [krɛ:m] |

groats (barley ~, etc.)	kroupy (ž mn)	[kroupɪ]
flour	mouka (ž)	[mouka]
canned food	konzerva (ž)	[konzɛrva]

cornflakes	kukuřičné vločky (ž mn)	[kukurʒɪtʃnɛ: vlotʃkɪ]
honey	med (m)	[mɛt]
jam	džem (m)	[dʒem]
chewing gum	žvýkačka (ž)	[ʒvi:katʃka]

53. Drinks

water	voda (ž)	[voda]
drinking water	pitná voda (ž)	[pɪtna: voda]
mineral water	minerální voda (ž)	[mɪnɛra:lni: voda]

still (adj)	neperlivý	[nɛpɛrlɪvi:]
carbonated (adj)	perlivý	[pɛrlɪvi:]
sparkling (adj)	perlivý	[pɛrlɪvi:]
ice	led (m)	[lɛt]
with ice	s ledem	[s lɛdɛm]

non-alcoholic (adj)	nealkoholický	[nɛalkoholɪtski:]
soft drink	nealkoholický nápoj (m)	[nɛalkoholɪtski: na:poj]
refreshing drink	osvěžující nápoj (m)	[osveʒuji:tsi na:poj]
lemonade	limonáda (ž)	[lɪmona:da]

liquors	alkoholické nápoje (m mn)	[alkoholɪtskɛ: na:pojɛ]
wine	víno (s)	[vi:no]
white wine	bílé víno (s)	[bi:lɛ: vi:no]
red wine	červené víno (s)	[tʃɛrvɛnɛ: vi:no]
liqueur	likér (m)	[lɪkɛ:r]
champagne	šampaňské (s)	[ʃampaɲskɛ:]

vermouth	**vermut** (m)	[vɛrmut]
whiskey	**whisky** (ž)	[vɪskɪ]
vodka	**vodka** (ž)	[votka]
gin	**džin** (m)	[dʒɪn]
cognac	**koňak** (m)	[konʲak]
rum	**rum** (m)	[rum]

coffee	**káva** (ž)	[ka:va]
black coffee	**černá káva** (ž)	[tʃɛrna: ka:va]
coffee with milk	**bílá káva** (ž)	[bi:la: ka:va]
cappuccino	**kapučíno** (s)	[kaputʃi:no]
instant coffee	**rozpustná káva** (ž)	[rozpustna: ka:va]

milk	**mléko** (s)	[mlɛ:ko]
cocktail	**koktail** (m)	[koktajl]
milkshake	**mléčný koktail** (m)	[mlɛtʃni: koktajl]

juice	**šťáva** (ž), **džus** (m)	[ʃtʲa:va], [dʒus]
tomato juice	**rajčatová šťáva** (ž)	[rajtʃatova: ʃtʲa:va]
orange juice	**pomerančový džus** (m)	[pomɛrantʃovi: dʒus]
freshly squeezed juice	**vymačkaná šťáva** (ž)	[vɪmatʃkana: ʃtʲa:va]

beer	**pivo** (s)	[pɪvo]
light beer	**světlé pivo** (s)	[svetlɛ: pɪvo]
dark beer	**tmavé pivo** (s)	[tmavɛ: pɪvo]

tea	**čaj** (m)	[tʃaj]
black tea	**černý čaj** (m)	[tʃɛrni: tʃaj]
green tea	**zelený čaj** (m)	[zɛlɛni: tʃaj]

54. Vegetables

vegetables	**zelenina** (ž)	[zɛlɛnɪna]
greens	**zelenina** (ž)	[zɛlɛnɪna]

tomato	**rajské jablíčko** (s)	[rajskɛ: jabli:tʃko]
cucumber	**okurka** (ž)	[okurka]
carrot	**mrkev** (ž)	[mrkɛf]
potato	**brambory** (ž mn)	[bramborɪ]
onion	**cibule** (ž)	[tsɪbulɛ]
garlic	**česnek** (m)	[tʃɛsnɛk]

cabbage	**zelí** (s)	[zɛli:]
cauliflower	**květák** (m)	[kveta:k]
Brussels sprouts	**růžičková kapusta** (ž)	[ruːʒɪtʃkova: kapusta]
broccoli	**brokolice** (ž)	[brokolɪtsɛ]

beet	**červená řepa** (ž)	[tʃɛrvena: rʒɛpa]
eggplant	**lilek** (m)	[lɪlɛk]
zucchini	**cukina, cuketa** (ž)	[tsukɪna], [tsuketa]

| pumpkin | tykev (ž) | [tɪkɛf] |
| turnip | vodní řepa (ž) | [vodni: rʒɛpa] |

parsley	petržel (ž)	[pɛtrʒel]
dill	kopr (m)	[kopr]
lettuce	salát (m)	[sala:t]
celery	celer (m)	[ʦɛlɛr]
asparagus	chřest (m)	[xrʃɛst]
spinach	špenát (m)	[ʃpɛna:t]

pea	hrách (m)	[hra:x]
beans	boby (m mn)	[bobɪ]
corn (maize)	kukuřice (ž)	[kukurʒɪʦɛ]
kidney bean	fazole (ž)	[fazolɛ]

bell pepper	pepř (m)	[pɛprʃ]
radish	ředkvička (ž)	[rʒɛtkvɪʧka]
artichoke	artyčok (m)	[artɪʧok]

55. Fruits. Nuts

fruit	ovoce (s)	[ovoʦɛ]
apple	jablko (s)	[jablko]
pear	hruška (ž)	[hruʃka]
lemon	citrón (m)	[ʦɪtro:n]
orange	pomeranč (m)	[pomɛranʧ]
strawberry (garden ~)	zahradní jahody (ž mn)	[zahradni: jahodɪ]

mandarin	mandarinka (ž)	[mandarɪŋka]
plum	švestka (ž)	[ʃvɛstka]
peach	broskev (ž)	[broskɛf]
apricot	meruňka (ž)	[mɛrunʲka]
raspberry	maliny (ž mn)	[malɪnɪ]
pineapple	ananas (m)	[ananas]

banana	banán (m)	[bana:n]
watermelon	vodní meloun (m)	[vodni: mɛloun]
grape	hroznové víno (s)	[hroznovɛ: vi:no]
sour cherry	višně (ž)	[vɪʃne]
sweet cherry	třešně (ž)	[trʃɛʃne]
melon	cukrový meloun (m)	[ʦukrovi: mɛloun]

grapefruit	grapefruit (m)	[grɛjpfru:t]
avocado	avokádo (s)	[avoka:do]
papaya	papája (ž)	[papa:ja]
mango	mango (s)	[mango]
pomegranate	granátové jablko (s)	[grana:tovɛ: jablko]

| redcurrant | červený rybíz (m) | [ʧɛrvɛnɪ: rɪbi:z] |
| blackcurrant | černý rybíz (m) | [ʧɛrni: rɪbi:z] |

gooseberry	angrešt (m)	[angrɛʃt]
bilberry	borůvky (ž mn)	[boru:fkɪ]
blackberry	ostružiny (ž mn)	[ostruʒɪnɪ]

raisin	hrozinky (ž mn)	[hrozɪŋkɪ]
fig	fík (m)	[fi:k]
date	datle (ž)	[datlɛ]

peanut	burský oříšek (m)	[burski: orʒi:ʃɛk]
almond	mandle (ž)	[mandlɛ]
walnut	vlašský ořech (m)	[vlaʃski: orʒɛx]
hazelnut	lískový ořech (m)	[li:skovi: orʒɛx]
coconut	kokos (m)	[kokos]
pistachios	pistácie (ž)	[pɪsta:tsɪe]

56. Bread. Candy

bakers' confectionery (pastry)	cukroví (s)	[ʦukrovi:]
bread	chléb (m)	[xlɛ:p]
cookies	sušenky (ž mn)	[suʃɛŋkɪ]

chocolate (n)	čokoláda (ž)	[tʃokola:da]
chocolate (as adj)	čokoládový	[tʃokola:dovi:]
candy (wrapped)	bonbón (m)	[bonbo:n]
cake (e.g., cupcake)	zákusek (m)	[za:kusɛk]
cake (e.g., birthday ~)	dort (m)	[dort]

| pie (e.g., apple ~) | koláč (m) | [kola:tʃ] |
| filling (for cake, pie) | nádivka (ž) | [na:dɪfka] |

jam (whole fruit jam)	zavařenina (ž)	[zavarʒɛnɪna]
marmalade	marmeláda (ž)	[marmɛla:da]
wafers	oplatky (mn)	[oplatkɪ]
ice-cream	zmrzlina (ž)	[zmrzlɪna]
pudding	pudink (m)	[pudɪŋk]

57. Spices

salt	sůl (ž)	[su:l]
salty (adj)	slaný	[slani:]
to salt (vt)	solit	[solɪt]

black pepper	černý pepř (m)	[tʃɛrni: pɛprʃ]
red pepper (milled ~)	červená paprika (ž)	[tʃɛrvɛna: paprɪka]
mustard	hořčice (ž)	[horʃtʃɪtsɛ]
horseradish	křen (m)	[krʃɛn]
condiment	ochucovadlo (s)	[oxutsovadlo]

spice	**koření** (s)	[korʒɛni:]
sauce	**omáčka** (ž)	[oma:tʃka]
vinegar	**ocet** (m)	[otsɛt]
anise	**anýz** (m)	[ani:z]
basil	**bazalka** (ž)	[bazalka]
cloves	**hřebíček** (m)	[hrʒɛbi:tʃɛk]
ginger	**zázvor** (m)	[za:zvor]
coriander	**koriandr** (m)	[korɪandr]
cinnamon	**skořice** (ž)	[skorʒɪtsɛ]
sesame	**sezam** (m)	[sɛzam]
bay leaf	**bobkový list** (m)	[bopkovi: lɪst]
paprika	**paprika** (ž)	[paprɪka]
caraway	**kmín** (m)	[kmi:n]
saffron	**šafrán** (m)	[ʃafra:n]

PERSONAL INFORMATION. FAMILY

Publishing

name (first name)	jméno (s)	[jmɛ:no]
surname (last name)	příjmení (s)	[prʃi:jmɛni:]
date of birth	datum (s) narození	[datum narozɛni:]
place of birth	místo (s) narození	[mi:sto narozɛni:]

nationality	národnost (ž)	[na:rodnost]
place of residence	bydliště (s)	[bɪdlɪʃte]
country	země (ž)	[zɛmnɛ]
profession (occupation)	povolání (s)	[povola:ni:]

gender, sex	pohlaví (s)	[pohlavi:]
height	postava (ž)	[postava]
weight	váha (ž)	[va:ha]

mother	matka (ž)	[matka]
father	otec (m)	[otɛts]
son	syn (m)	[sɪn]
daughter	dcera (ž)	[dtsɛra]

younger daughter	nejmladší dcera (ž)	[nɛjmladʃi: dtsɛra]
younger son	nejmladší syn (m)	[nɛjmladʃi: sɪn]
eldest daughter	nejstarší dcera (ž)	[nɛjstarʃi: dtsɛra]
eldest son	nejstarší syn (m)	[nɛjstarʃi: sɪn]

brother	bratr (m)	[bratr]
elder brother	starší bratr (m)	[starʃi: bratr]
younger brother	mladší bratr (m)	[mladʃi: bratr]
sister	sestra (ž)	[sɛstra]
elder sister	starší sestra (ž)	[starʃi: sɛstra]
younger sister	mladší sestra (ž)	[mladʃi: sɛstra]

cousin (masc.)	bratranec (m)	[bratranɛts]
cousin (fem.)	sestřenice (ž)	[sɛstrʃɛnɪtsɛ]
mom, mommy	maminka (ž)	[mamɪŋka]
dad, daddy	táta (m)	[ta:ta]
parents	rodiče (m mn)	[rodɪtʃɛ]
child	dítě (s)	[di:te]
children	děti (ž mn)	[detɪ]
grandmother	babička (ž)	[babɪtʃka]
grandfather	dědeček (m)	[dodɛtʃɛk]

grandson	vnuk (m)	[vnuk]
granddaughter	vnučka (ž)	[vnutʃka]
grandchildren	vnuci (m mn)	[vnutsɪ]

uncle	strýc (m)	[striːts]
aunt	teta (ž)	[tɛta]
nephew	synovec (m)	[sɪnovɛts]
niece	neteř (ž)	[nɛtɛrʃ]

mother-in-law (wife's mother)	tchyně (ž)	[txɪne]
father-in-law (husband's father)	tchán (m)	[txaːn]
son-in-law (daughter's husband)	zeť (m)	[zɛtʲ]
stepmother	nevlastní matka (ž)	[nɛvlastniː matka]
stepfather	nevlastní otec (m)	[nɛvlastniː otɛts]
infant	kojenec (m)	[kojɛnɛts]
baby (infant)	nemluvně (s)	[nɛmluvne]
little boy, kid	děcko (s)	[detsko]

wife	žena (ž)	[ʒena]
husband	muž (m)	[muʃ]
spouse (husband)	manžel (m)	[manʒel]
spouse (wife)	manželka (ž)	[manʒelka]

married (masc.)	ženatý	[ʒenatiː]
married (fem.)	vdaná	[vdanaː]
single (unmarried)	svobodný	[svobodniː]
bachelor	mládenec (m)	[mlaːdɛnɛts]
divorced (masc.)	rozvedený	[rozvɛdɛniː]
widow	vdova (ž)	[vdova]
widower	vdovec (m)	[vdovɛts]

relative	příbuzný (m)	[prʃiːbuzniː]
close relative	blízký příbuzný (m)	[bliːskiː prʃiːbuzniː]
distant relative	vzdálený příbuzný (m)	[vzdaːlɛni prʃiːbuzniː]
relatives	příbuzenstvo (s)	[prʃiːbuzɛnstvo]

orphan (boy or girl)	sirotek (m, ž)	[sɪrotɛk]
orphan (boy)	sirotek (m)	[sɪrotɛk]
orphan (girl)	sirotek (ž)	[sɪrotɛk]
guardian (of a minor)	poručník (m)	[porutʃniːk]
to adopt (a boy)	adoptovat	[adoptovat]
to adopt (a girl)	adoptovat dívku	[adoptovat difku]

60. Friends. Coworkers

| friend (masc.) | přítel (m) | [prʃiːtɛl] |
| friend (fem.) | přítelkyně (ž) | [prʃiːtɛlkɪne] |

| friendship | přátelství (s) | [prʃaːtɛlstviː] |
| to be friends | kamarádit | [kamaraːdɪt] |

buddy (masc.)	kamarád (m)	[kamaraːt]
buddy (fem.)	kamarádka (ž)	[kamaraːtka]
partner	partner (m)	[partnɛr]

chief (boss)	šéf (m)	[ʃɛːf]
superior (n)	vedoucí (m)	[vɛdoutsiː]
owner, proprietor	vlastník (m)	[vlastniːk]
subordinate (n)	podřízený (m)	[podrʒiːzɛniː]
colleague	kolega (m)	[kolɛga]

acquaintance (person)	známý (m)	[znaːmiː]
fellow traveler	spolucestující (m)	[spolutsɛstujiːtsi]
classmate	spolužák (m)	[spoluʒaːk]

neighbor (masc.)	soused (m)	[sousɛt]
neighbor (fem.)	sousedka (ž)	[sousɛtka]
neighbors	sousedé (m mn)	[sousɛdɛː]

HUMAN BODY. MEDICINE

T&P Books Publishing

61. Head

head	**hlava** (ž)	[hlava]
face	**obličej** (ž)	[oblɪtʃɛj]
nose	**nos** (m)	[nos]
mouth	**ústa** (s mn)	[uːsta]
eye	**oko** (s)	[oko]
eyes	**oči** (s mn)	[otʃɪ]
pupil	**zornice** (ž)	[zornɪtsɛ]
eyebrow	**obočí** (s)	[obotʃiː]
eyelash	**řasa** (ž)	[rʒasa]
eyelid	**víčko** (s)	[viːtʃko]
tongue	**jazyk** (m)	[jazɪk]
tooth	**zub** (m)	[zup]
lips	**rty** (m mn)	[rtɪ]
cheekbones	**lícní kosti** (ž mn)	[liːtsni: kostɪ]
gum	**dáseň** (ž)	[daːsɛnʲ]
palate	**patro** (s)	[patro]
nostrils	**chřípí** (s)	[xrʃiːpiː]
chin	**brada** (ž)	[brada]
jaw	**čelist** (ž)	[tʃɛlɪst]
cheek	**tvář** (ž)	[tvaːrʃ]
forehead	**čelo** (s)	[tʃɛlo]
temple	**spánek** (s)	[spaːnɛk]
ear	**ucho** (s)	[uxo]
back of the head	**týl** (m)	[tiːl]
neck	**krk** (m)	[krk]
throat	**hrdlo** (s)	[hrdlo]
hair	**vlasy** (m mn)	[vlasɪ]
hairstyle	**účes** (m)	[uːtʃɛs]
haircut	**střih** (m)	[strʃɪx]
wig	**paruka** (ž)	[paruka]
mustache	**vousy** (m mn)	[vousɪ]
beard	**plnovous** (m)	[plnovous]
to have (a beard, etc.)	**nosit**	[nosɪt]
braid	**cop** (m)	[tsop]
sideburns	**licousy** (m mn)	[lɪtsousɪ]
red-haired (adj)	**zrzavý**	[zrzaviː]
gray (hair)	**šedlvý**	[ʃɛdɪviː]

148

| bald (adj) | lysý | [lɪsi:] |
| bald patch | lysina (ž) | [lɪsɪna] |

| ponytail | ocas (m) | [oʦas] |
| bangs | ofina (ž) | [ofɪna] |

62. Human body

| hand | ruka (ž) | [ruka] |
| arm | ruka (ž) | [ruka] |

finger	prst (m)	[prst]
toe	prst (m) na noze	[prst na nozɛ]
thumb	palec (m)	[palɛʦ]
little finger	malíček (m)	[mali:ʧɛk]
nail	nehet (m)	[nɛhɛt]

fist	pěst (ž)	[pest]
palm	dlaň (ž)	[dlanj]
wrist	zápěstí (s)	[za:pɛsti:]
forearm	předloktí (s)	[prʃɛdlokti:]

| elbow | loket (m) | [lokɛt] |
| shoulder | rameno (s) | [ramɛno] |

leg	noha (ž)	[noha]
foot	chodidlo (s)	[xodɪdlo]
knee	koleno (s)	[kolɛno]
calf (part of leg)	lýtko (s)	[li:tko]

| hip | stehno (s) | [stɛhno] |
| heel | pata (ž) | [pata] |

body	tělo (s)	[telo]
stomach	břicho (s)	[brʒɪxo]
chest	prsa (s mn)	[prsa]
breast	prs (m)	[prs]
flank	bok (m)	[bok]
back	záda (s mn)	[za:da]

| lower back | kříž (m) | [krʃi:ʃ] |
| waist | pás (m) | [pa:s] |

navel (belly button)	pupek (m)	[pupɛk]
buttocks	hýždě (ž mn)	[hi:ʒde]
bottom	zadek (m)	[zadɛk]

beauty mark	mateřské znaménko (s)	[matɛrʃkɛ: znamɛ:ŋko]
tattoo	tetování (s)	[tɛtova:ni:]
scar	jizva (ž)	[jɪzva]

63. Diseases

sickness	nemoc (ž)	[nɛmoʦ]
to be sick	být nemocný	[bi:t nɛmoʦni:]
health	zdraví (s)	[zdravi:]

runny nose (coryza)	rýma (ž)	[ri:ma]
tonsillitis	angína (ž)	[angi:na]
cold (illness)	nachlazení (s)	[naxlazɛni:]
to catch a cold	nachladit se	[naxladɪt sɛ]

bronchitis	bronchitida (ž)	[bronxɪti:da]
pneumonia	zápal (m) plic	[za:pal plɪʦ]
flu, influenza	chřipka (ž)	[xrʃɪpka]

nearsighted (adj)	krátkozraký	[kra:tkozraki:]
farsighted (adj)	dalekozraký	[dalɛkozraki:]
strabismus (crossed eyes)	šilhavost (ž)	[ʃɪlhavost]
cross-eyed (adj)	šilhavý	[ʃɪlhavi:]
cataract	šedý zákal (m)	[ʃɛdi: za:kal]
glaucoma	zelený zákal (m)	[zɛlɛni: za:kal]

stroke	mozková mrtvice (ž)	[moskova: mrtvɪʦɛ]
heart attack	infarkt (m)	[ɪnfarkt]
myocardial infarction	infarkt (m) myokardu	[ɪnfarkt mɪokardu]
paralysis	obrna (ž)	[obrna]
to paralyze (vt)	paralyzovat	[paralɪzovat]

allergy	alergie (ž)	[alɛrgɪe]
asthma	astma (s)	[astma]
diabetes	cukrovka (ž)	[ʦukrofka]

toothache	bolení (s) zubů	[bolɛni: zubu:]
caries	zubní kaz (m)	[zubni: kaz]

diarrhea	průjem (m)	[pru:jɛm]
constipation	zácpa (ž)	[za:ʦpa]
stomach upset	žaludeční potíže (ž mn)	[ʒaludɛʧni: poti:ʒe]
food poisoning	otrava (ž)	[otrava]
to get food poisoning	otrávit se	[otra:vɪt sɛ]

arthritis	artritida (ž)	[artrɪtɪda]
rickets	rachitida (ž)	[raxɪtɪda]
rheumatism	revmatismus (m)	[rɛvmatɪzmus]
atherosclerosis	ateroskleróza (ž)	[atɛrosklɛro:za]

gastritis	gastritida (ž)	[gastrɪtɪda]
appendicitis	apendicitida (ž)	[apɛndɪʦɪtɪda]
cholecystitis	zánět (m) žlučníku	[za:net ʒluʧni:ku]
ulcer	vřed (m)	[vrʒɛt]
measles	spalničky (ž mn)	[spalnɪʧki:]

rubella (German measles)	zardĕnky (ž mn)	[zardeŋkɪ]
jaundice	žloutenka (ž)	[ʒloutɛŋka]
hepatitis	hepatitida (ž)	[hɛpatɪtɪda]

schizophrenia	schizofrenie (ž)	[sxɪzofrɛnɪe]
rabies (hydrophobia)	vzteklina (ž)	[vstɛklɪna]
neurosis	neuróza (ž)	[nɛuro:za]
concussion	otřes (m) mozku	[otrʃɛs mosku]

cancer	rakovina (ž)	[rakovɪna]
sclerosis	skleróza (ž)	[sklɛro:za]
multiple sclerosis	roztroušená skleróza (ž)	[roztrouʃɛna: sklɛro:za]

alcoholism	alkoholismus (m)	[alkoholɪzmus]
alcoholic (n)	alkoholik (m)	[alkoholɪk]
syphilis	syfilida (ž)	[sɪfɪlɪda]
AIDS	AIDS (m)	[ajts]

tumor	nádor (m)	[na:dor]
malignant (adj)	zhoubný	[zhoubni:]
benign (adj)	nezhoubný	[nɛzhoubni:]

fever	zimnice (ž)	[zɪmnɪtsɛ]
malaria	malárie (ž)	[mala:rɪe]
gangrene	gangréna (ž)	[gangrɛ:na]
seasickness	mořská nemoc (ž)	[morʃska: nɛmots]
epilepsy	padoucnice (ž)	[padoutsnɪtsɛ]

epidemic	epidemie (ž)	[ɛpɪdɛmɪe]
typhus	tyf (m)	[tɪf]
tuberculosis	tuberkulóza (ž)	[tubɛrkulo:za]
cholera	cholera (ž)	[xolɛra]
plague (bubonic ~)	mor (m)	[mor]

64. Symptoms. Treatments. Part 1

symptom	příznak (m)	[prʃi:znak]
temperature	teplota (ž)	[tɛplota]
high temperature (fever)	vysoká teplota (ž)	[vɪsoka: tɛplota]
pulse (heartbeat)	tep (m)	[tɛp]

dizziness (vertigo)	závrať (ž)	[za:vratʲ]
hot (adj)	horký	[horki:]
shivering	mrazení (s)	[mrazɛni:]
pale (e.g., ~ face)	bledý	[blɛdi:]

cough	kašel (m)	[kaʃɛl]
to cough (vi)	kašlat	[kaʃlat]
to sneeze (vi)	kýchat	[ki:xat]
faint	mdloby (ž mn)	[mdlobɪ]

151

to faint (vi)	**upadnout do mdlob**	[upadnout do mdlop]
bruise (hématome)	**modřina** (ž)	[modrʒɪna]
bump (lump)	**boule** (ž)	[boulɛ]
to bang (bump)	**uhodit se**	[uhodɪt sɛ]
contusion (bruise)	**pohmožděnina** (ž)	[pohmoʒdenɪna]
to get a bruise	**uhodit se**	[uhodɪt sɛ]
to limp (vi)	**kulhat**	[kulhat]
dislocation	**vykloubení** (s)	[vɪkloubɛni:]
to dislocate (vt)	**vykloubit**	[vɪkloubɪt]
fracture	**zlomenina** (ž)	[zlomɛnɪna]
to have a fracture	**dostat zlomeninu**	[dostat zlomɛnɪnu]
cut (e.g., paper ~)	**říznutí** (s)	[rʒi:znuti:]
to cut oneself	**říznout se**	[rʒi:znout sɛ]
bleeding	**krvácení** (s)	[krva:ʦɛni:]
burn (injury)	**popálenina** (ž)	[popa:lɛnɪna]
to get burned	**spálit se**	[spa:lɪt sɛ]
to prick (vt)	**píchnout**	[pi:xnout]
to prick oneself	**píchnout se**	[pi:xnout sɛ]
to injure (vt)	**pohmoždit**	[pohmoʒdɪt]
injury	**pohmoždění** (s)	[pohmoʒdeni:]
wound	**rána** (ž)	[ra:na]
trauma	**úraz** (m)	[u:raz]
to be delirious	**blouznit**	[blouznɪt]
to stutter (vi)	**zajíkat se**	[zaji:kat sɛ]
sunstroke	**úpal** (m)	[u:pal]

65. Symptoms. Treatments. Part 2

pain, ache	**bolest** (ž)	[bolɛst]
splinter (in foot, etc.)	**tříska** (ž)	[trʃi:ska]
sweat (perspiration)	**pot** (m)	[pot]
to sweat (perspire)	**potit se**	[potɪt sɛ]
vomiting	**zvracení** (s)	[zvraʦɛni:]
convulsions	**křeče** (ž mn)	[krʃɛtʃɛ]
pregnant (adj)	**těhotná**	[tehotna:]
to be born	**narodit se**	[narodɪt sɛ]
delivery, labor	**porod** (m)	[porot]
to deliver (~ a baby)	**rodit**	[rodɪt]
abortion	**umělý potrat** (m)	[umneli: potrat]
breathing, respiration	**dýchání** (s)	[di:xa:ni:]
in-breath (inhalation)	**vdech** (m)	[vdɛx]
out-breath (exhalation)	**výdech** (m)	[vi:dɛx]

to exhale (breathe out)	vydechnout	[vɪdɛxnout]
to inhale (vi)	nadechnout se	[nadɛxnout sɛ]

disabled person	invalida (m)	[ɪnvalɪda]
cripple	mrzák (m)	[mrza:k]
drug addict	narkoman (m)	[narkoman]

deaf (adj)	hluchý	[hluxi:]
mute (adj)	němý	[nemi:]
deaf mute (adj)	hluchoněmý	[hluxonemi:]

mad, insane (adj)	šílený	[ʃi:lɛni:]
madman	šílenec (m)	[ʃi:lɛnɛts]
(demented person)		
madwoman	šílenec (ž)	[ʃi:lɛnɛts]
to go insane	zešílet	[zɛʃi:lɛt]

gene	gen (m)	[gɛn]
immunity	imunita (ž)	[ɪmunɪta]
hereditary (adj)	dědičný	[dedɪtʃni:]
congenital (adj)	vrozený	[vrozɛni:]

virus	virus (m)	[vɪrus]
microbe	mikrob (m)	[mɪkrop]
bacterium	baktérie (ž)	[baktɛ:rɪe]
infection	infekce (ž)	[ɪnfɛktsɛ]

66. Symptoms. Treatments. Part 3

hospital	nemocnice (ž)	[nɛmotsnɪtsɛ]
patient	pacient (m)	[patsɪent]

diagnosis	diagnóza (ž)	[dɪagno:za]
cure	léčení (s)	[lɛ:tʃɛni:]
medical treatment	léčba (ž)	[lɛ:tʃba]
to get treatment	léčit se	[lɛ:tʃɪt sɛ]
to treat (~ a patient)	léčit	[lɛ:tʃɪt]
to nurse (look after)	ošetřovat	[oʃɛtrʃovat]
care (nursing ~)	ošetřování (s)	[oʃɛtrʃova:ni:]

operation, surgery	operace (ž)	[opɛratsɛ]
to bandage (head, limb)	obvázat	[obva:zat]
bandaging	obvazování (s)	[obvazova:ni:]

vaccination	očkování (s)	[otʃkova:ni:]
to vaccinate (vt)	dělat očkování	[delat otʃkova:ni:]
injection, shot	injekce (ž)	[ɪnjɛktsɛ]
to give an injection	dávat injekci	[da:vat ɪnjɛktsɪ]
attack	záchvat (m)	[za:xvat]
amputation	amputace (ž)	[amputatsɛ]

to amputate (vt)	amputovat	[amputovat]
coma	kóma (s)	[ko:ma]
to be in a coma	být v kómatu	[bi:t v ko:matu]
intensive care	reanimace (ž)	[rɛanɪmaʦɛ]

to recover (~ from flu)	uzdravovat se	[uzdravovat sɛ]
condition (patient's ~)	stav (m)	[staf]
consciousness	vědomí (s)	[vedomi:]
memory (faculty)	paměť (ž)	[pamnetʲ]

to pull out (tooth)	trhat	[trhat]
filling	plomba (ž)	[plomba]
to fill (a tooth)	plombovat	[plombovat]

| hypnosis | hypnóza (ž) | [hɪpno:za] |
| to hypnotize (vt) | hypnotizovat | [hɪpnotɪzovat] |

67. Medicine. Drugs. Accessories

medicine, drug	lék (m)	[lɛ:k]
remedy	prostředek (m)	[prostrʃɛdɛk]
to prescribe (vt)	předepsat	[prʒɛdɛpsat]
prescription	recept (m)	[rɛʦɛpt]

tablet, pill	tableta (ž)	[tablɛta]
ointment	mast (ž)	[mast]
ampule	ampule (ž)	[ampulɛ]
mixture, solution	mixtura (ž)	[mɪkstura]
syrup	sirup (m)	[sɪrup]
capsule	pilulka (ž)	[pɪlulka]
powder	prášek (m)	[pra:ʃɛk]

gauze bandage	obvaz (m)	[obvaz]
cotton wool	vata (ž)	[vata]
iodine	jód (m)	[jo:t]

| Band-Aid | leukoplast (m) | [lɛukoplast] |
| eyedropper | pipeta (ž) | [pɪpɛta] |

| thermometer | teploměr (m) | [tɛplomner] |
| syringe | injekční stříkačka (ž) | [ɪnjɛkʧni: strʃi:kaʧka] |

| wheelchair | vozík (m) | [vozi:k] |
| crutches | berle (ž mn) | [bɛrlɛ] |

painkiller	anestetikum (s)	[anɛstɛtɪkum]
laxative	projímadlo (s)	[proji:madlo]
spirits (ethanol)	líh (m)	[li:x]
medicinal herbs	bylina (ž)	[bɪlɪna]
herbal (~ tea)	bylinný	[bɪlɪnni:]

APARTMENT

T&P Books Publishing

68. Apartment

apartment	**byt** (m)	[bɪt]
room	**pokoj** (m)	[pokoj]
bedroom	**ložnice** (ž)	[loʒnɪtsɛ]
dining room	**jídelna** (ž)	[ji:dɛlna]
living room	**přijímací pokoj** (m)	[prʃɪji:matsi: pokoj]
study (home office)	**pracovna** (ž)	[pratsovna]
entry room	**předsíň** (ž)	[prʃɛtsi:nʲ]
bathroom (room with a bath or shower)	**koupelna** (ž)	[koupɛlna]
half bath	**záchod** (m)	[za:xot]
ceiling	**strop** (m)	[strop]
floor	**podlaha** (ž)	[podlaha]
corner	**kout** (m)	[kout]

69. Furniture. Interior

furniture	**nábytek** (m)	[na:bɪtɛk]
table	**stůl** (m)	[stu:l]
chair	**židle** (ž)	[ʒɪdlɛ]
bed	**lůžko** (s)	[lu:ʃko]
couch, sofa	**pohovka** (ž)	[pohofka]
armchair	**křeslo** (s)	[krʃɛslo]
bookcase	**knihovna** (ž)	[knɪhovna]
shelf	**police** (ž)	[polɪtsɛ]
wardrobe	**skříň** (ž)	[skrʃi:nʲ]
coat rack (wall-mounted ~)	**předsíňový věšák** (m)	[prʃɛdsi:novi: vɛʃa:k]
coat stand	**stojanový věšák** (m)	[stojanovi: vɛʃa:k]
bureau, dresser	**prádelník** (m)	[pra:dɛlni:k]
coffee table	**konferenční stolek** (m)	[konfɛrɛntʃni: stolɛk]
mirror	**zrcadlo** (s)	[zrtsadlo]
carpet	**koberec** (m)	[kobɛrɛts]
rug, small carpet	**kobereček** (m)	[kobɛrɛtʃɛk]
fireplace	**krb** (m)	[krp]
candle	**svíce** (ž)	[svi:tsɛ]
candlestick	**svícen** (m)	[svi:tsɛn]

drapes	**záclony** (ž mn)	[za:tslonɪ]
wallpaper	**tapety** (ž mn)	[tapɛtɪ]
blinds (jalousie)	**žaluzie** (ž)	[ʒaluzɪe]

table lamp	**stolní lampa** (ž)	[stolni: lampa]
wall lamp (sconce)	**svítidlo** (s)	[svi:tɪdlo]
floor lamp	**stojací lampa** (ž)	[stojatsi: lampa]
chandelier	**lustr** (m)	[lustr]

leg (of chair, table)	**noha** (ž)	[noha]
armrest	**područka** (ž)	[podruʧka]
back (backrest)	**opěradlo** (s)	[operadlo]
drawer	**zásuvka** (ž)	[za:sufka]

70. Bedding

bedclothes	**ložní prádlo** (s)	[loʒni: pra:dlo]
pillow	**polštář** (m)	[polʃta:rʃ]
pillowcase	**povlak** (m) **na polštář**	[povlak na polʃta:rʒ]
duvet, comforter	**deka** (ž)	[dɛka]
sheet	**prostěradlo** (s)	[prosteradlo]
bedspread	**přikrývka** (ž)	[prʃɪkri:fka]

71. Kitchen

kitchen	**kuchyně** (ž)	[kuxɪne]
gas	**plyn** (m)	[plɪn]
gas stove (range)	**plynový sporák** (m)	[plɪnovi: spora:k]
electric stove	**elektrický sporák** (m)	[ɛlɛktrɪtski: spora:k]
oven	**trouba** (ž)	[trouba]
microwave oven	**mikrovlnná pec** (ž)	[mɪkrovlnna: pɛts]

refrigerator	**lednička** (ž)	[lɛdnɪʧka]
freezer	**mrazicí komora** (ž)	[mrazɪtsi: komora]
dishwasher	**myčka** (ž) **nádobí**	[mɪʧka na:dobi:]

meat grinder	**mlýnek** (m) **na maso**	[mli:nɛk na maso]
juicer	**odšťavňovač** (m)	[otʃtʲavnʲovaʧ]
toaster	**opékač** (m) **topinek**	[opɛ:kaʧ topɪnɛk]
mixer	**mixér** (m)	[mɪksɛ:r]

coffee machine	**kávovar** (m)	[ka:vovar]
coffee pot	**konvice** (ž) **na kávu**	[konvɪtsɛ na ka:vu]
coffee grinder	**mlýnek** (m) **na kávu**	[mli:nɛk na ka:vu]

kettle	**čajník** (m)	[ʧajni:k]
teapot	**čajová konvice** (ž)	[ʧajova: konvɪtsɛ]
lid	**poklička** (ž)	[poklɪʧka]

tea strainer	cedítko (s)	[tsɛdiːtko]
spoon	lžíce (ž)	[ʒiːtsɛ]
teaspoon	kávová lžička (ž)	[kaːvova: ʒɪtʃka]
soup spoon	polévková lžíce (ž)	[polɛːfkova: ʒiːtsɛ]
fork	vidlička (ž)	[vɪdlɪtʃka]
knife	nůž (m)	[nuːʃ]

tableware (dishes)	nádobí (s)	[naːdobi:]
plate (dinner ~)	talíř (m)	[taliːrʃ]
saucer	talířek (m)	[taliːrʒɛk]

shot glass	sklenička (ž)	[sklɛnɪtʃka]
glass (tumbler)	sklenice (ž)	[sklɛnɪtsɛ]
cup	šálek (m)	[ʃaːlɛk]

sugar bowl	cukřenka (ž)	[tsukrʃɛŋka]
salt shaker	solnička (ž)	[solnɪtʃka]
pepper shaker	pepřenka (ž)	[pɛprʃɛŋka]
butter dish	nádobka (ž) na máslo	[naːdopka na ma:slo]

stock pot (soup pot)	hrnec (m)	[hrnɛts]
frying pan (skillet)	pánev (ž)	[pa:nɛf]
ladle	naběračka (ž)	[naberatʃka]
colander	cedník (m)	[tsɛdni:k]
tray (serving ~)	podnos (m)	[podnos]

bottle	láhev (ž)	[la:hɛf]
jar (glass)	sklenice (ž)	[sklɛnɪtsɛ]
can	plechovka (ž)	[plɛxofka]

bottle opener	otvírač (m) lahví	[otvi:ratʃ lahvi:]
can opener	otvírač (m) konzerv	[otvi:ratʃ konzɛrf]
corkscrew	vývrtka (ž)	[vi:vrtka]
filter	filtr (m)	[fɪltr]
to filter (vt)	filtrovat	[fɪltrovat]

| trash, garbage (food waste, etc.) | odpadky (m mn) | [otpatki:] |
| trash can (kitchen ~) | kbelík (m) na odpadky | [gbɛli:k na otpatkɪ] |

72. Bathroom

bathroom	koupelna (ž)	[koupɛlna]
water	voda (ž)	[voda]
faucet	kohout (m)	[kohout]
hot water	teplá voda (ž)	[tɛpla: voda]
cold water	studená voda (ž)	[studɛna: voda]

| toothpaste | zubní pasta (ž) | [zubni: pasta] |
| to brush one's teeth | čistit si zuby | [tʃɪstɪt sɪ zubɪ] |

toothbrush	kartáček (m) na zuby	[karta:tʃɛk na zubɪ]
to shave (vi)	holit se	[holɪt sɛ]
shaving foam	pěna (ž) na holení	[pena na holɛni:]
razor	holicí strojek (m)	[holɪtsi: strojɛk]

to wash (one's hands, etc.)	mýt	[mi:t]
to take a bath	mýt se	[mi:t sɛ]
shower	sprcha (ž)	[sprxa]
to take a shower	sprchovat se	[sprxovat sɛ]

bathtub	vana (ž)	[vana]
toilet (toilet bowl)	záchodová mísa (ž)	[za:xodova: mi:sa]
sink (washbasin)	umývadlo (s)	[umi:vadlo]

| soap | mýdlo (m) | [mi:dlo] |
| soap dish | miska (ž) na mýdlo | [mɪska na mi:dlo] |

sponge	mycí houba (ž)	[mɪtsi: houba]
shampoo	šampon (m)	[ʃampon]
towel	ručník (m)	[rutʃni:k]
bathrobe	župan (m)	[ʒupan]

laundry (laundering)	praní (s)	[prani:]
washing machine	pračka (ž)	[pratʃka]
to do the laundry	prát	[pra:t]
laundry detergent	prací prášek (m)	[pratsi: pra:ʃɛk]

73. Household appliances

TV set	televizor (m)	[tɛlɛvɪzor]
tape recorder	magnetofon (m)	[magnɛtofon]
VCR (video recorder)	videomagnetofon (m)	[vɪdɛomagnɛtofon]
radio	přijímač (m)	[prʃɪji:matʃ]
player (CD, MP3, etc.)	přehrávač (m)	[prʃɛhra:vatʃ]

video projector	projektor (m)	[projɛktor]
home movie theater	domácí biograf (m)	[doma:tsi: bɪograf]
DVD player	DVD přehrávač (m)	[dɛvɛdɛ prʃɛhra:vatʃ]
amplifier	zesilovač (m)	[zɛsɪlovatʃ]
video game console	hrací přístroj (m)	[hratsi: prʃi:stroj]

video camera	videokamera (ž)	[vɪdɛokamɛra]
camera (photo)	fotoaparát (m)	[fotoapara:t]
digital camera	digitální fotoaparát (m)	[dɪgɪta:lni: fotoapara:t]

vacuum cleaner	vysavač (m)	[vɪsavatʃ]
iron (e.g., steam ~)	žehlička (ž)	[ʒehlɪtʃka]
ironing board	žehlicí prkno (s)	[ʒehlɪtsi: prkno]
telephone	telefon (m)	[tɛlɛfon]
cell phone	mobilní telefon (m)	[mobɪlni: tɛlɛfon]

| typewriter | psací stroj (m) | [psatsi: stroj] |
| sewing machine | šicí stroj (m) | [ʃɪtsi: stroj] |

microphone	mikrofon (m)	[mɪkrofon]
headphones	sluchátka (s mn)	[sluxa:tka]
remote control (TV)	ovládač (m)	[ovla:datʃ]

CD, compact disc	CD disk (m)	[tsɛ:dɛ: dɪsk]
cassette, tape	kazeta (ž)	[kazɛta]
vinyl record	deska (ž)	[dɛska]

THE EARTH. WEATHER

T&P Books Publishing

74. Outer space

space	kosmos (m)	[kosmos]
space (as adj)	kosmický	[kosmɪtski:]
outer space	kosmický prostor (m)	[kosmɪtski: prostor]
world, universe	vesmír (m)	[vɛsmi:r]
world	svět (m)	[svet]
galaxy	galaxie (ž)	[galaksɪe]
star	hvězda (ž)	[hvezda]
constellation	souhvězdí (s)	[souhvɛzdi:]
planet	planeta (ž)	[planɛta]
satellite	družice (ž)	[druʒɪtsɛ]
meteorite	meteorit (m)	[mɛtɛorɪt]
comet	kometa (ž)	[komɛta]
asteroid	asteroid (m)	[astɛroɪt]
orbit	oběžná dráha (ž)	[obeʒna: dra:ha]
to revolve	otáčet se	[ota:tʃɛt sɛ]
(~ around the Earth)		
atmosphere	atmosféra (ž)	[atmosfɛ:ra]
the Sun	Slunce (s)	[sluntsɛ]
solar system	sluneční soustava (ž)	[slunɛtʃni: soustava]
solar eclipse	sluneční zatmění (s)	[slunɛtʃni: zatmneni:]
the Earth	Země (ž)	[zɛmnɛ]
the Moon	Měsíc (m)	[mnesi:ts]
Mars	Mars (m)	[mars]
Venus	Venuše (ž)	[vɛnuʃɛ]
Jupiter	Jupiter (m)	[jupɪtɛr]
Saturn	Saturn (m)	[saturn]
Mercury	Merkur (m)	[mɛrkur]
Uranus	Uran (m)	[uran]
Neptune	Neptun (m)	[nɛptun]
Pluto	Pluto (s)	[pluto]
Milky Way	Mléčná dráha (ž)	[mlɛ:tʃna: dra:ha]
Great Bear (Ursa Major)	Velká medvědice (ž)	[vɛlka: mɛdvedɪtsɛ]
North Star	Polárka (ž)	[pola:rka]
Martian	Marťan (m)	[martʲan]
extraterrestrial (n)	mimozemšťan (m)	[mɪmozɛmʃtʲan]

| alien | vetřelec (m) | [vɛtrʃɛlɛts] |
| flying saucer | létající talíř (m) | [lɛ:taji:tsi: tali:rʃ] |

spaceship	kosmická loď (ž)	[kosmɪtska: loti]
space station	orbitální stanice (ž)	[orbɪta:lni: stanɪtsɛ]
blast-off	start (m)	[start]

engine	motor (m)	[motor]
nozzle	tryska (ž)	[trɪska]
fuel	palivo (s)	[palɪvo]

cockpit, flight deck	kabina (ž)	[kabɪna]
antenna	anténa (ž)	[antɛ:na]
porthole	okénko (s)	[okɛ:ŋko]
solar panel	sluneční baterie (ž)	[slunɛtʃni: batɛrɪe]
spacesuit	skafandr (m)	[skafandr]

| weightlessness | beztížný stav (m) | [bɛzti:ʒni: staf] |
| oxygen | kyslík (m) | [kɪsli:k] |

| docking (in space) | spojení (s) | [spojɛni:] |
| to dock (vi, vt) | spojovat se | [spojovat sɛ] |

observatory	observatoř (ž)	[opsɛrvatorʃ]
telescope	teleskop (m)	[tɛlɛskop]
to observe (vt)	pozorovat	[pozorovat]
to explore (vt)	zkoumat	[skoumat]

75. The Earth

the Earth	Země (ž)	[zɛmnɛ]
the globe (the Earth)	zeměkoule (ž)	[zɛmnekoulɛ]
planet	planeta (ž)	[planɛta]

atmosphere	atmosféra (ž)	[atmosfɛ:ra]
geography	zeměpis (m)	[zɛmnepɪs]
nature	příroda (ž)	[prʃi:roda]

globe (table ~)	glóbus (m)	[glo:bus]
map	mapa (ž)	[mapa]
atlas	atlas (m)	[atlas]

Europe	Evropa (ž)	[ɛvropa]
Asia	Asie (ž)	[azɪe]
Africa	Afrika (ž)	[afrɪka]
Australia	Austrálie (ž)	[austra:lɪe]

America	Amerika (ž)	[amɛrɪka]
North America	Severní Amerika (ž)	[sɛvɛrni: amɛrɪka]
South America	Jižní Amerika (ž)	[jɪʒni: amɛrɪka]

| Antarctica | **Antarktida** (ž) | [antarkti:da] |
| the Arctic | **Arktida** (ž) | [arktɪda] |

76. Cardinal directions

north	**sever** (m)	[sɛvɛr]
to the north	**na sever**	[na sɛvɛr]
in the north	**na severu**	[na sɛvɛru]
northern (adj)	**severní**	[sɛvɛrni:]

south	**jih** (m)	[jɪx]
to the south	**na jih**	[na jɪx]
in the south	**na jihu**	[na jɪhu]
southern (adj)	**jižní**	[jɪʒni:]

west	**západ** (m)	[za:pat]
to the west	**na západ**	[na za:pat]
in the west	**na západě**	[na za:pade]
western (adj)	**západní**	[za:padni:]

east	**východ** (m)	[vi:xot]
to the east	**na východ**	[na vi:xot]
in the east	**na východě**	[na vi:xode]
eastern (adj)	**východní**	[vi:xodni:]

77. Sea. Ocean

sea	**moře** (s)	[morʒɛ]
ocean	**oceán** (m)	[oʦɛa:n]
gulf (bay)	**záliv** (m)	[za:lɪf]
straits	**průliv** (m)	[pru:lɪf]

land (solid ground)	**země** (ž)	[zɛmnɛ]
continent (mainland)	**pevnina** (ž)	[pɛvnɪna]
island	**ostrov** (m)	[ostrof]
peninsula	**poloostrov** (m)	[poloostrof]
archipelago	**souostroví** (s)	[souostrovi:]

bay, cove	**zátoka** (ž)	[za:toka]
harbor	**přístav** (m)	[prʃi:staf]
lagoon	**laguna** (ž)	[lagu:na]
cape	**mys** (m)	[mɪs]

atoll	**atol** (m)	[atol]
reef	**útes** (m)	[u:tɛs]
coral	**korál** (m)	[kora:l]
coral reef	**korálový útes** (m)	[kora:lovi: u:tɛs]
deep (adj)	**hluboký**	[hluboki:]

depth (deep water)	hloubka (ž)	[hloupka]
abyss	hlubina (ž)	[hlubɪna]
trench (e.g., Mariana ~)	prohlubeň (ž)	[prohlubɛnʲ]
current (Ocean ~)	proud (m)	[prout]
to surround (bathe)	omývat	[omi:vat]
shore	břeh (m)	[brʒɛx]
coast	pobřeží (s)	[pobrʒɛʒi:]
flow (flood tide)	příliv (m)	[prʃi:lɪf]
ebb (ebb tide)	odliv (m)	[odlɪf]
shoal	mělčina (ž)	[mneltʃɪna]
bottom (~ of the sea)	dno (s)	[dno]
wave	vlna (ž)	[vlna]
crest (~ of a wave)	hřbet (m) vlny	[hrʒbɛt vlnɪ]
spume (sea foam)	pěna (ž)	[pena]
storm (sea storm)	bouřka (ž)	[bourʃka]
hurricane	hurikán (m)	[hurɪka:n]
tsunami	tsunami (s)	[tsunamɪ]
calm (dead ~)	bezvětří (s)	[bɛzvetrʃi:]
quiet, calm (adj)	klidný	[klɪdni:]
pole	pól (m)	[po:l]
polar (adj)	polární	[pola:rni:]
latitude	šířka (ž)	[ʃi:rʃka]
longitude	délka (ž)	[dɛ:lka]
parallel	rovnoběžka (ž)	[rovnobeʃka]
equator	rovník (m)	[rovni:k]
sky	obloha (ž)	[obloha]
horizon	horizont (m)	[horɪzont]
air	vzduch (m)	[vzdux]
lighthouse	maják (m)	[maja:k]
to dive (vi)	potápět se	[pota:pet sɛ]
to sink (ab. boat)	potopit se	[potopɪt sɛ]
treasures	bohatství (s)	[bohatstvi:]

78. Seas' and Oceans' names

Atlantic Ocean	Atlantický oceán (m)	[atlantɪtski: oʦɛa:n]
Indian Ocean	Indický oceán (m)	[ɪndɪtski: oʦɛa:n]
Pacific Ocean	Tichý oceán (m)	[tɪxi: oʦɛa:n]
Arctic Ocean	Severní ledový oceán (m)	[sɛverni: lɛdovi: oʦɛa:n]
Black Sea	Černé moře (s)	[tʃɛrnɛ: morʒɛ]
Red Sea	Rudé moře (s)	[rudɛ: morʒɛ]

| Yellow Sea | Žluté moře (s) | [ʒlutɛ: morʒɛ] |
| White Sea | Bílé moře (s) | [bi:lɛ: morʒɛ] |

Caspian Sea	Kaspické moře (s)	[kaspɪtskɛ: morʒɛ]
Dead Sea	Mrtvé moře (s)	[mrtvɛ: morʒɛ]
Mediterranean Sea	Středozemní moře (s)	[strʃɛdozɛmni: morʒɛ]

| Aegean Sea | Egejské moře (s) | [ɛgɛjskɛ: morʒɛ] |
| Adriatic Sea | Jaderské moře (s) | [jadɛrskɛ: morʒɛ] |

Arabian Sea	Arabské moře (s)	[arapskɛ: morʒɛ]
Sea of Japan	Japonské moře (s)	[japonskɛ: morʒɛ]
Bering Sea	Beringovo moře (s)	[bɛrɪngovo morʒɛ]
South China Sea	Jihočínské moře (s)	[jɪhotʃi:nskɛ: morʒɛ]

Coral Sea	Korálové moře (s)	[kora:lovɛ: morʒɛ]
Tasman Sea	Tasmanovo moře (s)	[tasmanovo morʒɛ]
Caribbean Sea	Karibské moře (s)	[karɪpskɛ: morʒɛ]

| Barents Sea | Barentsovo moře (s) | [barɛntsovo morʒɛ] |
| Kara Sea | Karské moře (s) | [karskɛ: morʒɛ] |

North Sea	Severní moře (s)	[sɛvɛrni: morʒɛ]
Baltic Sea	Baltské moře (s)	[baltskɛ: morʒɛ]
Norwegian Sea	Norské moře (s)	[norskɛ: morʒɛ]

79. Mountains

mountain	hora (ž)	[hora]
mountain range	horské pásmo (s)	[horskɛ: pa:smo]
mountain ridge	horský hřbet (m)	[horski: hrʒbɛt]

summit, top	vrchol (m)	[vrxol]
peak	štít (m)	[ʃti:t]
foot (~ of the mountain)	úpatí (s)	[u:pati:]
slope (mountainside)	svah (m)	[svax]

volcano	sopka (ž)	[sopka]
active volcano	činná sopka (ž)	[tʃɪnna: sopka]
dormant volcano	vyhaslá sopka (ž)	[vɪhasla: sopka]

eruption	výbuch (m)	[vi:bux]
crater	kráter (m)	[kra:tɛr]
magma	magma (ž)	[magma]
lava	láva (ž)	[la:va]
molten (~ lava)	rozžhavený	[rozʒhavɛni:]

canyon	kaňon (m)	[kanʲon]
gorge	soutěska (ž)	[souteska]
crevice	rozsedlina (ž)	[rozsɛdlɪna]

abyss (chasm)	propast (ž)	[propast]
pass, col	průsmyk (m)	[pru:smɪk]
plateau	plató (s)	[plato:]
cliff	skála (ž)	[ska:la]
hill	kopec (m)	[kopɛts]

glacier	ledovec (m)	[lɛdovɛts]
waterfall	vodopád (m)	[vodopa:t]
geyser	vřídlo (s)	[vrʒi:dlo]
lake	jezero (s)	[jɛzɛro]

plain	rovina (ž)	[rovɪna]
landscape	krajina (ž)	[krajɪna]
echo	ozvěna (ž)	[ozvena]

alpinist	horolezec (m)	[horolɛzɛts]
rock climber	horolezec (m)	[horolɛzɛts]
to conquer (in climbing)	dobývat	[dobi:vat]
climb (an easy ~)	výstup (m)	[vi:stup]

80. Mountains names

The Alps	Alpy (mn)	[alpɪ]
Mont Blanc	Mont Blanc (m)	[monblaŋ]
The Pyrenees	Pyreneje (mn)	[pɪrɛnɛjɛ]

The Carpathians	Karpaty (mn)	[karpatɪ]
The Ural Mountains	Ural (m)	[ural]
The Caucasus Mountains	Kavkaz (m)	[kafkaz]
Mount Elbrus	Elbrus (m)	[ɛlbrus]

The Altai Mountains	Altaj (m)	[altaj]
The Tian Shan	Ťan-šan (ž)	[tʲan-ʃan]
The Pamir Mountains	Pamír (m)	[pami:r]
The Himalayas	Himaláje (mn)	[hɪmala:jɛ]
Mount Everest	Mount Everest (m)	[mount ɛvɛrɛst]

| The Andes | Andy (mn) | [andɪ] |
| Mount Kilimanjaro | Kilimandžáro (s) | [kɪlɪmandʒa:ro] |

81. Rivers

river	řeka (ž)	[rʒɛka]
spring (natural source)	pramen (m)	[pramɛn]
riverbed (river channel)	koryto (s)	[korɪto]
basin (river valley)	povodí (s)	[povodi:]
to flow into …	vlévat se	[vlɛ:vat sɛ]
tributary	přítok (m)	[prʃi:tok]

bank (of river)	břeh (m)	[brʒɛx]
current (stream)	proud (m)	[prout]
downstream (adv)	po proudu	[po proudu]
upstream (adv)	proti proudu	[protɪ proudu]

inundation	povodeň (ž)	[povodɛnʲ]
flooding	záplava (ž)	[za:plava]
to overflow (vi)	rozlévat se	[rozlɛ:vat sɛ]
to flood (vt)	zaplavovat	[zaplavovat]

| shallow (shoal) | mělčina (ž) | [mnɛltʃɪna] |
| rapids | peřej (ž) | [pɛrʒɛj] |

dam	přehrada (ž)	[prʃɛhrada]
canal	průplav (m)	[pru:plaf]
reservoir (artificial lake)	vodní nádrž (ž)	[vodni: na:drʃ]
sluice, lock	zdymadlo (s)	[zdɪmadlo]

water body (pond, etc.)	vodojem (m)	[vodojɛm]
swamp (marshland)	bažina (ž)	[baʒɪna]
bog, marsh	slať (ž)	[slatʲ]
whirlpool	vír (m)	[vi:r]

stream (brook)	potok (m)	[potok]
drinking (ab. water)	pitný	[pɪtni:]
fresh (~ water)	sladký	[slatki:]

| ice | led (m) | [lɛt] |
| to freeze over (ab. river, etc.) | zamrznout | [zamrznout] |

82. Rivers' names

| Seine | Seina (ž) | [se:na] |
| Loire | Loira (ž) | [loa:ra] |

Thames	Temže (ž)	[tɛmʒe]
Rhine	Rýn (m)	[ri:n]
Danube	Dunaj (m)	[dunaj]

Volga	Volha (ž)	[volha]
Don	Don (m)	[don]
Lena	Lena (ž)	[lɛna]

Yellow River	Chuang-chež (ž)	[xuan-xɛ]
Yangtze	Jang-c'-ťiang (ž)	[jang-tsɛ-tʲang]
Mekong	Mekong (m)	[mɛkong]
Ganges	Ganga (ž)	[ganga]
Nile River	Nil (m)	[nɪl]
Congo River	Kongo (s)	[kongo]

Okavango River	Okavango (s)	[okavango]
Zambezi River	Zambezi (ž)	[zambɛzɪ]
Limpopo River	Limpopo (s)	[lɪmpopo]
Mississippi River	Mississippi (ž)	[mɪsɪsɪpɪ]

83. Forest

| forest, wood | les (m) | [lɛs] |
| forest (as adj) | lesní | [lɛsni:] |

thick forest	houština (ž)	[houʃtɪna]
grove	háj (m)	[ha:j]
forest clearing	mýtina (ž)	[mi:tɪna]

| thicket | houští (s) | [houʃti:] |
| scrubland | křoví (s) | [krʃovi:] |

| footpath (troddenpath) | stezka (ž) | [stɛska] |
| gully | rokle (ž) | [roklɛ] |

tree	strom (m)	[strom]
leaf	list (m)	[lɪst]
leaves (foliage)	listí (s)	[lɪsti:]

fall of leaves	padání (s) listí	[pada:ni: lɪsti:]
to fall (ab. leaves)	opadávat	[opada:vat]
top (of the tree)	vrchol (m)	[vrxol]

branch	větev (ž)	[vetɛf]
bough	suk (m)	[suk]
bud (on shrub, tree)	pupen (m)	[pupɛn]
needle (of pine tree)	jehla (ž)	[jɛhla]
pine cone	šiška (ž)	[ʃɪʃka]

tree hollow	dutina (ž)	[dutɪna]
nest	hnízdo (s)	[hni:zdo]
burrow (animal hole)	doupě (s)	[doupe]

trunk	kmen (m)	[kmɛn]
root	kořen (m)	[korʒɛn]
bark	kůra (ž)	[ku:ra]
moss	mech (m)	[mɛx]

| to uproot (remove trees or tree stumps) | klučit | [klutʃɪt] |

to chop down	kácet	[ka:tsɛt]
to deforest (vt)	odlesnit	[odlesnɪt]
tree stump	pařez (m)	[parʒɛz]
campfire	oheň (m)	[ohɛnʲ]
forest fire	požár (m)	[poʒa:r]

to extinguish (vt)	hasit	[hasɪt]
forest ranger	hajný (m)	[hajni:]
protection	ochrana (ž)	[oxrana]
to protect (~ nature)	chránit	[xra:nɪt]
poacher	pytlák (m)	[pɪtla:k]
steel trap	past (ž)	[past]

| to gather, to pick (vt) | sbírat | [zbi:rat] |
| to lose one's way | zabloudit | [zabloudɪt] |

84. Natural resources

natural resources	přírodní zdroje (m mn)	[prʃi:rodni: zdrojɛ]
minerals	užitkové nerosty (m mn)	[uʒɪtkovɛ: nɛrostɪ]
deposits	ložisko (s)	[loʒɪsko]
field (e.g., oilfield)	naleziště (s)	[nalezɪʃte]

to mine (extract)	dobývat	[dobi:vat]
mining (extraction)	těžba (ž)	[teʒba]
ore	ruda (ž)	[ruda]
mine (e.g., for coal)	důl (m)	[du:l]
shaft (mine ~)	šachta (ž)	[ʃaxta]
miner	horník (m)	[horni:k]

| gas (natural ~) | plyn (m) | [plɪn] |
| gas pipeline | plynovod (m) | [plɪnovot] |

oil (petroleum)	ropa (ž)	[ropa]
oil pipeline	ropovod (m)	[ropovot]
oil well	ropová věž (ž)	[ropova: veʃ]
derrick (tower)	vrtná věž (ž)	[vrtna: veʃ]
tanker	tanková loď (ž)	[taŋkova: lotʲ]

sand	písek (m)	[pi:sɛk]
limestone	vápenec (m)	[va:pɛnɛʦ]
gravel	štěrk (m)	[ʃterk]
peat	rašelina (ž)	[raʃɛlɪna]
clay	hlína (ž)	[hli:na]
coal	uhlí (s)	[uhli:]

iron (ore)	železo (s)	[ʒelɛzo]
gold	zlato (s)	[zlato]
silver	stříbro (s)	[strʃi:bro]
nickel	nikl (m)	[nɪkl]
copper	měď (ž)	[mnetʲ]

zinc	zinek (m)	[zɪnɛk]
manganese	mangan (m)	[mangan]
mercury	rtuť (ž)	[rtutʲ]
lead	olovo (s)	[olovo]

mineral	minerál (m)	[mɪnɛra:l]
crystal	krystal (m)	[krɪstal]
marble	mramor (m)	[mramor]
uranium	uran (m)	[uran]

85. Weather

weather	počasí (s)	[potʃasi:]
weather forecast	předpověď (ž) počasí	[prʃɛtpovetʲ potʃasi:]
temperature	teplota (ž)	[tɛplota]
thermometer	teploměr (m)	[tɛplomner]
barometer	barometr (m)	[baromɛtr]

humid (adj)	vlhký	[vlxki:]
humidity	vlhkost (ž)	[vlxkost]
heat (extreme ~)	horko (s)	[horko]
hot (torrid)	horký	[horki:]
it's hot	horko	[horko]

| it's warm | teplo | [tɛplo] |
| warm (moderately hot) | teplý | [tɛpli:] |

it's cold	je zima	[jɛ zɪma]
cold (adj)	studený	[studɛni:]
sun	slunce (s)	[sluntsɛ]
to shine (vi)	svítit	[svi:tɪt]
sunny (day)	sluneční	[slunɛtʃni:]
to come up (vi)	vzejít	[vzɛji:t]
to set (vi)	zapadnout	[zapadnout]

cloud	mrak (m)	[mrak]
cloudy (adj)	oblačný	[oblatʃni:]
rain cloud	mračno (s)	[mratʃno]
somber (gloomy)	pochmurný	[poxmurni:]

rain	déšť (m)	[dɛ:ʃtʲ]
it's raining	prší	[prʃi:]
rainy (~ day, weather)	deštivý	[dɛʃtɪvi:]
to drizzle (vi)	mrholit	[mrholɪt]

pouring rain	liják (m)	[lɪja:k]
downpour	liják (m)	[lɪja:k]
heavy (e.g., ~ rain)	silný	[sɪlni:]
puddle	kaluž (ž)	[kaluʃ]
to get wet (in rain)	moknout	[moknout]

fog (mist)	mlha (ž)	[mlha]
foggy	mlhavý	[mlhavi:]
snow	sníh (m)	[sni:x]
it's snowing	sněží	[snɛʒi:]

86. Severe weather. Natural disasters

thunderstorm	bouřka (ž)	[bourʃka]
lightning (~ strike)	blesk (m)	[blɛsk]
to flash (vi)	blýskat se	[bliːskat sɛ]
thunder	hřmění (s)	[hrʒmneniː]
to thunder (vi)	hřmít	[hrʒmiːt]
it's thundering	hřmí	[hrʒmiː]
hail	kroupy (ž mn)	[kroupɪ]
it's hailing	padají kroupy	[padajiː kroupɪ]
to flood (vt)	zaplavit	[zaplavɪt]
flood, inundation	povodeň (ž)	[povodɛnʲ]
earthquake	zemětřesení (s)	[zɛmnetrʃɛsɛniː]
tremor, shoke	otřes (m)	[otrʃɛs]
epicenter	epicentrum (s)	[ɛpɪʦɛntrum]
eruption	výbuch (m)	[viːbux]
lava	láva (ž)	[laːva]
twister	smršť (ž)	[smrʃtʲ]
tornado	tornádo (s)	[tornaːdo]
typhoon	tajfun (m)	[tajfun]
hurricane	hurikán (m)	[hurɪkaːn]
storm	bouřka (ž)	[bourʃka]
tsunami	tsunami (s)	[tsunamɪ]
cyclone	cyklón (m)	[ʦikloːn]
bad weather	nečas (m)	[nɛtʃas]
fire (accident)	požár (m)	[poʒaːr]
disaster	katastrofa (ž)	[katastrofa]
meteorite	meteorit (m)	[mɛtɛorɪt]
avalanche	lavina (ž)	[lavɪna]
snowslide	lavina (ž)	[lavɪna]
blizzard	metelice (ž)	[mɛtɛlɪʦɛ]
snowstorm	vánice (ž)	[vaːnɪʦɛ]

FAUNA

T&P Books Publishing

87. Mammals. Predators

predator	**šelma** (ž)	[ʃɛlma]
tiger	**tygr** (m)	[tɪgr]
lion	**lev** (m)	[lɛf]
wolf	**vlk** (m)	[vlk]
fox	**liška** (ž)	[lɪʃka]
jaguar	**jaguár** (m)	[jagua:r]
leopard	**levhart** (m)	[lɛvhart]
cheetah	**gepard** (m)	[gɛpart]
black panther	**panter** (m)	[pantɛr]
puma	**puma** (ž)	[puma]
snow leopard	**pardál** (m)	[parda:l]
lynx	**rys** (m)	[rɪs]
coyote	**kojot** (m)	[kojot]
jackal	**šakal** (m)	[ʃakal]
hyena	**hyena** (ž)	[hɪena]

88. Wild animals

animal	**zvíře** (s)	[zvi:rʒɛ]
beast (animal)	**zvíře** (s)	[zvi:rʒɛ]
squirrel	**veverka** (ž)	[vɛvɛrka]
hedgehog	**ježek** (m)	[jɛʒek]
hare	**zajíc** (m)	[zaji:ts]
rabbit	**králík** (m)	[kra:li:k]
badger	**jezevec** (m)	[jɛzɛvɛts]
raccoon	**mýval** (m)	[mi:val]
hamster	**křeček** (m)	[krʃɛtʃɛk]
marmot	**svišť** (m)	[svɪʃtʲ]
mole	**krtek** (m)	[krtɛk]
mouse	**myš** (ž)	[mɪʃ]
rat	**krysa** (ž)	[krɪsa]
bat	**netopýr** (m)	[nɛtopi:r]
ermine	**hranostaj** (m)	[hranostaj]
sable	**sobol** (m)	[sobol]
marten	**kuna** (ž)	[kuna]

| weasel | lasice (ž) | [lasɪtsɛ] |
| mink | norek (m) | [norɛk] |

| beaver | bobr (m) | [bobr] |
| otter | vydra (ž) | [vɪdra] |

horse	kůň (m)	[kuːnʲ]
moose	los (m)	[los]
deer	jelen (m)	[jɛlɛn]
camel	velbloud (m)	[vɛlblout]

bison	bizon (m)	[bɪzon]
wisent	zubr (m)	[zubr]
buffalo	buvol (m)	[buvol]

zebra	zebra (ž)	[zɛbra]
antelope	antilopa (ž)	[antɪlopa]
roe deer	srnka (ž)	[srŋka]
fallow deer	daněk (m)	[danek]
chamois	kamzík (m)	[kamziːk]
wild boar	vepř (m)	[vɛprʃ]

whale	velryba (ž)	[vɛlrɪba]
seal	tuleň (m)	[tulɛnʲ]
walrus	mrož (m)	[mroʃ]
fur seal	lachtan (m)	[laxtan]
dolphin	delfín (m)	[dɛlfiːn]

bear	medvěd (m)	[mɛdvet]
polar bear	bílý medvěd (m)	[biːliː mɛdvet]
panda	panda (ž)	[panda]

monkey	opice (ž)	[opɪtsɛ]
chimpanzee	šimpanz (m)	[ʃɪmpanz]
orangutan	orangutan (m)	[orangutan]
gorilla	gorila (ž)	[gorɪla]
macaque	makak (m)	[makak]
gibbon	gibon (m)	[gɪbon]

| elephant | slon (m) | [slon] |
| rhinoceros | nosorožec (m) | [nosoroʒets] |

| giraffe | žirafa (ž) | [ʒɪrafa] |
| hippopotamus | hroch (m) | [hrox] |

| kangaroo | klokan (m) | [klokan] |
| koala (bear) | koala (ž) | [koala] |

mongoose	promyka (ž) indická	[promɪka ɪndɪtska:]
chinchilla	činčila (ž)	[tʃɪntʃɪla]
skunk	skunk (m)	[skuŋk]
porcupine	dikobraz (m)	[dɪkobras]

89. Domestic animals

cat	kočka (ž)	[kotʃka]
tomcat	kocour (m)	[kotsour]
dog	pes (m)	[pɛs]

horse	kůň (m)	[ku:nʲ]
stallion (male horse)	hřebec (m)	[hrʒɛbɛts]
mare	kobyla (ž)	[kobɪla]

cow	kráva (ž)	[kra:va]
bull	býk (m)	[bi:k]
ox	vůl (m)	[vu:l]

sheep (ewe)	ovce (ž)	[ovtsɛ]
ram	beran (m)	[bɛran]
goat	koza (ž)	[koza]
billy goat, he-goat	kozel (m)	[kozɛl]

| donkey | osel (m) | [osɛl] |
| mule | mul (m) | [mul] |

pig, hog	prase (s)	[prasɛ]
piglet	prasátko (s)	[prasa:tko]
rabbit	králík (m)	[kra:li:k]

| hen (chicken) | slepice (ž) | [slɛpɪtsɛ] |
| rooster | kohout (m) | [kohout] |

duck	kachna (ž)	[kaxna]
drake	kačer (m)	[katʃɛr]
goose	husa (ž)	[husa]

| tom turkey, gobbler | krocan (m) | [krotsan] |
| turkey (hen) | krůta (ž) | [kru:ta] |

domestic animals	domácí zvířata (s mn)	[doma:tsi: zvi:rʒata]
tame (e.g., ~ hamster)	ochočený	[oxotʃɛni:]
to tame (vt)	ochočovat	[oxotʃovat]
to breed (vt)	chovat	[xovat]

farm	farma (ž)	[farma]
poultry	drůbež (ž)	[dru:bɛʃ]
cattle	dobytek (m)	[dobɪtɛk]
herd (cattle)	stádo (s)	[sta:do]

stable	stáj (ž)	[sta:j]
pigpen	vepřín (m)	[vɛprʃi:n]
cowshed	kravín (m)	[kravi:n]
rabbit hutch	králíkárna (ž)	[kra:li:ka:rna]
hen house	kurník (m)	[kurni:k]

90. Birds

bird	pták (m)	[pta:k]
pigeon	holub (m)	[holup]
sparrow	vrabec (m)	[vrabɛts]
tit (great tit)	sýkora (ž)	[si:kora]
magpie	straka (ž)	[straka]

raven	havran (m)	[havran]
crow	vrána (ž)	[vra:na]
jackdaw	kavka (ž)	[kafka]
rook	polní havran (m)	[polni: havran]

duck	kachna (ž)	[kaxna]
goose	husa (ž)	[husa]
pheasant	bažant (m)	[baʒant]

eagle	orel (m)	[orɛl]
hawk	jestřáb (m)	[jɛstrʃa:p]
falcon	sokol (m)	[sokol]
vulture	sup (m)	[sup]
condor (Andean ~)	kondor (m)	[kondor]

swan	labuť (ž)	[labutʲ]
crane	jeřáb (m)	[jɛrʒa:p]
stork	čáp (m)	[tʃa:p]

parrot	papoušek (m)	[papouʃɛk]
hummingbird	kolibřík (m)	[kolɪbrʒi:k]
peacock	páv (m)	[pa:f]

ostrich	pštros (m)	[pʃtros]
heron	volavka (ž)	[volafka]
flamingo	plameňák (m)	[plamɛnʲa:k]
pelican	pelikán (m)	[pɛlɪka:n]

| nightingale | slavík (m) | [slavi:k] |
| swallow | vlaštovka (ž) | [vlaʃtofka] |

thrush	drozd (m)	[drozt]
song thrush	zpěvný drozd (m)	[spevni: drozt]
blackbird	kos (m)	[kos]

swift	rorejs (m)	[rorɛjs]
lark	skřivan (m)	[skrʃɪvan]
quail	křepel (m)	[krʃɛpɛl]

woodpecker	datel (m)	[datɛl]
cuckoo	kukačka (ž)	[kukatʃka]
owl	sova (ž)	[sova]
eagle owl	výr (m)	[vi:r]

wood grouse	tetřev (m) hlušec	[tɛtrʃɛv hluʃɛts]
black grouse	tetřev (m)	[tɛtrʃɛf]
partridge	koroptev (ž)	[koroptɛf]

starling	špaček (m)	[ʃpatʃɛk]
canary	kanár (m)	[kana:r]
hazel grouse	jeřábek (m)	[jɛrʒa:bɛk]
chaffinch	pěnkava (ž)	[peŋkava]
bullfinch	hejl (m)	[hɛjl]

seagull	racek (m)	[ratsɛk]
albatross	albatros (m)	[albatros]
penguin	tučňák (m)	[tutʃɲa:k]

91. Fish. Marine animals

bream	cejn (m)	[tsɛjn]
carp	kapr (m)	[kapr]
perch	okoun (m)	[okoun]
catfish	sumec (m)	[sumɛts]
pike	štika (ž)	[ʃtɪka]

| salmon | losos (m) | [losos] |
| sturgeon | jeseter (m) | [jɛsɛtɛr] |

herring	sleď (ž)	[slɛtʲ]
Atlantic salmon	losos (m)	[losos]
mackerel	makrela (ž)	[makrɛla]
flatfish	platýs (m)	[plati:s]

zander, pike perch	candát (m)	[tsanda:t]
cod	treska (ž)	[trɛska]
tuna	tuňák (m)	[tunʲa:k]
trout	pstruh (m)	[pstrux]

eel	úhoř (m)	[u:horʃ]
electric ray	rejnok (m) elektrický	[rɛjnok ɛlɛktrɪtski:]
moray eel	muréna (ž)	[murɛ:na]
piranha	piraňa (ž)	[pɪranʲja]

shark	žralok (m)	[ʒralok]
dolphin	delfín (m)	[dɛlfi:n]
whale	velryba (ž)	[vɛlrɪba]

crab	krab (m)	[krap]
jellyfish	medúza (ž)	[mɛdu:za]
octopus	chobotnice (ž)	[xobotnɪtsɛ]

| starfish | hvězdice (ž) | [hvezdɪtsɛ] |
| sea urchin | ježovka (ž) | [jɛʒofka] |

seahorse	mořský koníček (m)	[morʃski: koni:tʃɛk]
oyster	ústřice (ž)	[u:strʃɪtsɛ]
shrimp	kreveta (ž)	[krɛvɛta]
lobster	humr (m)	[humr]
spiny lobster	langusta (ž)	[langusta]

92. Amphibians. Reptiles

| snake | had (m) | [hat] |
| venomous (snake) | jedovatý | [jɛdovati:] |

viper	zmije (ž)	[zmɪjɛ]
cobra	kobra (ž)	[kobra]
python	krajta (ž)	[krajta]
boa	hroznýš (m)	[hrozni:ʃ]

grass snake	užovka (ž)	[uʒofka]
rattle snake	chřestýš (m)	[xrʃɛsti:ʃ]
anaconda	anakonda (ž)	[anakonda]

lizard	ještěrka (ž)	[jɛʃterka]
iguana	leguán (m)	[lɛgua:n]
monitor lizard	varan (m)	[varan]
salamander	mlok (m)	[mlok]
chameleon	chameleón (m)	[xamɛlɛo:n]
scorpion	štír (m)	[ʃti:r]

turtle	želva (ž)	[ʒelva]
frog	žába (ž)	[ʒa:ba]
toad	ropucha (ž)	[ropuxa]
crocodile	krokodýl (m)	[krokodi:l]

93. Insects

insect, bug	hmyz (m)	[hmɪz]
butterfly	motýl (m)	[moti:l]
ant	mravenec (m)	[mravɛnɛts]
fly	moucha (ž)	[mouxa]
mosquito	komár (m)	[koma:r]
beetle	brouk (m)	[brouk]

wasp	vosa (ž)	[vosa]
bee	včela (ž)	[vtʃɛla]
bumblebee	čmelák (m)	[tʃmɛla:k]
gadfly (botfly)	střeček (m)	[strʃɛtʃɛk]

| spider | pavouk (m) | [pavouk] |
| spiderweb | pavučina (ž) | [pavutʃɪna] |

dragonfly	vážka (ž)	[vaːʃka]
grasshopper	kobylka (ž)	[kobɪlka]
moth (night butterfly)	motýl (m)	[motiːl]

cockroach	šváb (m)	[ʃvaːp]
tick	klíště (s)	[kliːʃte]
flea	blecha (ž)	[blɛxa]
midge	muška (ž)	[muʃka]

locust	saranče (ž)	[sarantʃɛ]
snail	hlemýžď (m)	[hlɛmiːʒtʲ]
cricket	cvrček (m)	[tsvrtʃɛk]
lightning bug	svatojánská muška (ž)	[svatojaːnska: muʃka]
ladybug	slunéčko (s) sedmitečné	[slunɛːtʃko sɛdmɪtɛtʃnɛː]
cockchafer	chroust (m)	[xroust]

leech	piavice (ž)	[pɪavɪtsɛ]
caterpillar	housenka (ž)	[housɛŋka]
earthworm	červ (m)	[tʃɛrf]
larva	larva (ž)	[larva]

FLORA

T&P Books Publishing

tree	**strom** (m)	[strom]
deciduous (adj)	**listnatý**	[lɪstnati:]
coniferous (adj)	**jehličnatý**	[jɛhlɪtʃnati:]
evergreen (adj)	**stálezelená**	[sta:lɛzɛlɛna:]
apple tree	**jabloň** (ž)	[jablonʲ]
pear tree	**hruška** (ž)	[hruʃka]
sweet cherry tree	**třešně** (ž)	[trʃɛʃne]
sour cherry tree	**višně** (ž)	[vɪʃne]
plum tree	**švestka** (ž)	[ʃvɛstka]
birch	**bříza** (ž)	[brʒi:za]
oak	**dub** (m)	[dup]
linden tree	**lípa** (ž)	[li:pa]
aspen	**osika** (ž)	[osɪka]
maple	**javor** (m)	[javor]
spruce	**smrk** (m)	[smrk]
pine	**borovice** (ž)	[borovɪtsɛ]
larch	**modřín** (m)	[modrʒi:n]
fir tree	**jedle** (ž)	[jɛdlɛ]
cedar	**cedr** (m)	[tsɛdr]
poplar	**topol** (m)	[topol]
rowan	**jeřáb** (m)	[jɛrʒa:p]
willow	**jíva** (ž)	[ji:va]
alder	**olše** (ž)	[olʃɛ]
beech	**buk** (m)	[buk]
elm	**jilm** (m)	[jɪlm]
ash (tree)	**jasan** (m)	[jasan]
chestnut	**kaštan** (m)	[kaʃtan]
magnolia	**magnólie** (ž)	[magno:lɪe]
palm tree	**palma** (ž)	[palma]
cypress	**cypřiš** (m)	[tsɪprʃɪʃ]
mangrove	**mangróvie** (ž)	[mangro:vɪe]
baobab	**baobab** (m)	[baobap]
eucalyptus	**eukalypt** (m)	[ɛukalɪpt]
sequoia	**sekvoje** (ž)	[sɛkvojɛ]

95. Shrubs

| bush | keř (m) | [kɛrʃ] |
| shrub | křoví (s) | [krʃoviː] |

| grapevine | vinná réva (s) | [vɪnnaː reːva] |
| vineyard | vinice (ž) | [vɪnɪtsɛ] |

raspberry bush	maliny (ž mn)	[malɪnɪ]
blackcurrant bush	černý rybíz (m)	[tʃɛrni rɪbiːz]
redcurrant bush	červený rybíz (m)	[tʃɛrvɛni rɪbiːz]
gooseberry bush	angrešt (m)	[angrɛʃt]

acacia	akácie (ž)	[akaːtsɪe]
barberry	dřišťál (m)	[drʒɪʃtʲaːl]
jasmine	jasmín (m)	[jasmiːn]

juniper	jalovec (m)	[jalovɛts]
rosebush	růžový keř (m)	[ruːʒovɪ kɛrʃ]
dog rose	šípek (m)	[ʃiːpɛk]

96. Fruits. Berries

fruit	ovoce (s), plod (m)	[ovotsɛ], [plot]
fruits	ovoce (s mn)	[ovotsɛ]
apple	jablko (s)	[jablko]
pear	hruška (ž)	[hruʃka]
plum	švestka (ž)	[ʃvɛstka]

strawberry (garden ~)	zahradní jahody (ž mn)	[zahradniː jahodɪ]
sour cherry	višně (ž)	[vɪʃne]
sweet cherry	třešně (ž mn)	[trʃɛʃne]
grape	hroznové víno (s)	[hroznovɛː viːno]

raspberry	maliny (ž mn)	[malɪnɪ]
blackcurrant	černý rybíz (m)	[tʃɛrni rɪbiːz]
redcurrant	červený rybíz (m)	[tʃɛrvɛni rɪbiːz]
gooseberry	angrešt (m)	[angrɛʃt]
cranberry	klikva (ž)	[klɪkva]

orange	pomeranč (m)	[pomɛrantʃ]
mandarin	mandarinka (ž)	[mandarɪŋka]
pineapple	ananas (m)	[ananas]
banana	banán (m)	[banaːn]
date	datle (ž)	[datlɛ]

lemon	citrón (m)	[tsɪtroːn]
apricot	meruňka (ž)	[mɛrunʲka]
peach	broskev (ž)	[broskɛf]

kiwi	kiwi (s)	[kɪvɪ]
grapefruit	grapefruit (m)	[grɛjpfru:t]

berry	bobule (ž)	[bobulɛ]
berries	bobule (ž mn)	[bobulɛ]
cowberry	brusinky (ž mn)	[brusɪŋkɪ]
wild strawberry	jahody (ž mn)	[jahodɪ]
bilberry	borůvky (ž mn)	[boru:fkɪ]

97. Flowers. Plants

flower	květina (ž)	[kvetɪna]
bouquet (of flowers)	kytice (ž)	[kɪtɪtsɛ]

rose (flower)	růže (ž)	[ru:ʒe]
tulip	tulipán (m)	[tulɪpa:n]
carnation	karafiát (m)	[karafɪa:t]
gladiolus	mečík (m)	[mɛtʃi:k]

cornflower	chrpa (ž)	[xrpa]
harebell	zvoneček (m)	[zvonɛtʃɛk]
dandelion	pampeliška (ž)	[pampɛlɪʃka]
camomile	heřmánek (m)	[hɛrʒma:nɛk]

aloe	aloe (s)	[aloɛ]
cactus	kaktus (m)	[kaktus]
rubber plant, ficus	fíkus (m)	[fi:kus]

lily	lilie (ž)	[lɪlɪe]
geranium	gerânie (ž)	[gera:nɪe]
hyacinth	hyacint (m)	[hɪatsɪnt]

mimosa	citlivka (ž)	[tsɪtlɪfka]
narcissus	narcis (m)	[nartsɪs]
nasturtium	potočnice (ž)	[pototʃnɪtsɛ]

orchid	orchidej (ž)	[orxɪdɛj]
peony	pivoňka (ž)	[pɪvonʲka]
violet	fialka (ž)	[fɪalka]

pansy	maceška (ž)	[matsɛʃka]
forget-me-not	pomněnka (ž)	[pomnɛŋka]
daisy	sedmikráska (ž)	[sɛdmɪkra:ska]

poppy	mák (m)	[ma:k]
hemp	konopě (ž)	[konope]
mint	máta (ž)	[ma:ta]

lily of the valley	konvalinka (ž)	[konvalɪŋka]
snowdrop	sněženka (ž)	[sneʒeŋka]

nettle	kopřiva (ž)	[kopr∫ɪva]
sorrel	šťovík (m)	[∫ťovi:k]
water lily	leknín (m)	[lɛkni:n]
fern	kapradí (s)	[kapradi:]
lichen	lišejník (m)	[lɪ∫ɛjni:k]

conservatory (greenhouse)	oranžérie (ž)	[oranʒe:rɪe]
lawn	trávník (m)	[tra:vni:k]
flowerbed	květinový záhonek (m)	[kvetɪnovi: za:honɛk]

plant	rostlina (ž)	[rostlɪna]
grass	tráva (ž)	[tra:va]
blade of grass	stéblo (s) trávy	[stɛ:blo tra:vɪ]

leaf	list (m)	[lɪst]
petal	okvětní lístek (m)	[okvetni: li:stɛk]
stem	stéblo (s)	[stɛ:blo]
tuber	hlíza (ž)	[hli:za]

| young plant (shoot) | výhonek (m) | [vi:honɛk] |
| thorn | osten (m) | [ostɛn] |

to blossom (vi)	kvést	[kvɛ:st]
to fade, to wither	vadnout	[vadnout]
smell (odor)	vůně (ž)	[vu:ne]
to cut (flowers)	uříznout	[urʒi:znout]
to pick (a flower)	utrhnout	[utrhnout]

98. Cereals, grains

grain	obilí (s)	[obɪli:]
cereal crops	obilniny (ž mn)	[obɪlnɪnɪ]
ear (of barley, etc.)	klas (m)	[klas]

wheat	pšenice (ž)	[p∫enɪtse]
rye	žito (s)	[ʒɪto]
oats	oves (m)	[ovɛs]

| millet | jáhly (ž mn) | [ja:hlɪ] |
| barley | ječmen (m) | [jɛt∫mɛn] |

corn	kukuřice (ž)	[kukurʒɪtse]
rice	rýže (ž)	[ri:ʒe]
buckwheat	pohanka (ž)	[pohaŋka]

pea plant	hrách (m)	[hra:x]
kidney bean	fazole (ž)	[fazolɛ]
soy	sója (ž)	[so:ja]
lentil	čočka (ž)	[t∫ot∫ka]
beans (pulse crops)	boby (m mn)	[bobɪ]

COUNTRIES OF
THE WORLD

T&P Books Publishing

Afghanistan	**Afghánistán** (m)	[afgaːnɪstaːn]
Albania	**Albánie** (ž)	[albaːnɪe]
Argentina	**Argentina** (ž)	[argɛntɪna]
Armenia	**Arménie** (ž)	[armɛːnɪe]
Australia	**Austrálie** (ž)	[austraːlɪe]
Austria	**Rakousko** (s)	[rakousko]
Azerbaijan	**Ázerbájdžán** (m)	[aːzɛrbaːjdʒaːn]
The Bahamas	**Bahamy** (ž mn)	[bahamɪ]
Bangladesh	**Bangladéš** (m)	[bangladɛːʃ]
Belarus	**Bělorusko** (s)	[belorusko]
Belgium	**Belgie** (ž)	[bɛlgɪe]
Bolivia	**Bolívie** (ž)	[boliːvɪe]
Bosnia and Herzegovina	**Bosna a Hercegovina** (ž)	[bosna a hɛrtsɛgovɪna]
Brazil	**Brazílie** (ž)	[braziːlɪe]
Bulgaria	**Bulharsko** (s)	[bulharsko]
Cambodia	**Kambodža** (ž)	[kambodʒa]
Canada	**Kanada** (ž)	[kanada]
Chile	**Chile** (s)	[tʃɪlɛ]
China	**Čína** (ž)	[tʃiːna]
Colombia	**Kolumbie** (ž)	[kolumbɪe]
Croatia	**Chorvatsko** (s)	[xorvatsko]
Cuba	**Kuba** (ž)	[kuba]
Cyprus	**Kypr** (m)	[kɪpr]
Czech Republic	**Česko** (s)	[tʃɛsko]
Denmark	**Dánsko** (s)	[daːnsko]
Dominican Republic	**Dominikánská republika** (ž)	[domɪnɪkaːnska: rɛpublɪka]
Ecuador	**Ekvádor** (m)	[ɛkvaːdor]
Egypt	**Egypt** (m)	[ɛgɪpt]
England	**Anglie** (ž)	[anglɪe]
Estonia	**Estonsko** (s)	[ɛstonsko]
Finland	**Finsko** (s)	[fɪnsko]
France	**Francie** (ž)	[frantsɪe]
French Polynesia	**Francouzská Polynésie** (ž)	[frantsouska: polɪnɛːzɪe]
Georgia	**Gruzie** (ž)	[gruzɪe]
Germany	**Německo** (s)	[nemɛtsko]
Ghana	**Ghana** (ž)	[gana]
Great Britain	**Velká Británie** (ž)	[vɛlka: brɪtaːnɪe]
Greece	**Řecko** (s)	[rʒɛtsko]

| Haiti | **Haiti** (s) | [haɪtɪ] |
| Hungary | **Maďarsko** (s) | [madʲarsko] |

100. Countries. Part 2

Iceland	**Island** (m)	[ɪslant]
India	**Indie** (ž)	[ɪndɪe]
Indonesia	**Indonésie** (ž)	[ɪndonɛːzɪe]
Iran	**Írán** (m)	[iːraːn]
Iraq	**Irák** (m)	[ɪraːk]
Ireland	**Irsko** (s)	[ɪrsko]
Israel	**Izrael** (m)	[ɪzraɛl]
Italy	**Itálie** (ž)	[ɪtaːlɪe]

Jamaica	**Jamajka** (ž)	[jamajka]
Japan	**Japonsko** (s)	[japonsko]
Jordan	**Jordánsko** (s)	[jordaːnsko]
Kazakhstan	**Kazachstán** (m)	[kazaxstaːn]
Kenya	**Keňa** (ž)	[kɛnʲa]
Kirghizia	**Kyrgyzstán** (m)	[kɪrgɪstaːn]
Kuwait	**Kuvajt** (m)	[kuvajt]

Laos	**Laos** (m)	[laos]
Latvia	**Lotyšsko** (s)	[lotɪʃsko]
Lebanon	**Libanon** (m)	[lɪbanon]
Libya	**Libye** (ž)	[lɪbɪe]
Liechtenstein	**Lichtenštejnsko** (s)	[lɪxtɛnʃtɛjnsko]
Lithuania	**Litva** (ž)	[lɪtva]
Luxembourg	**Lucembursko** (s)	[luʦɛmbursko]

Macedonia (Republic of ~)	**Makedonie** (ž)	[makɛdonɪe]
Madagascar	**Madagaskar** (m)	[madagaskar]
Malaysia	**Malajsie** (ž)	[malajzɪe]
Malta	**Malta** (ž)	[malta]
Mexico	**Mexiko** (s)	[mɛksɪko]
Moldova, Moldavia	**Moldavsko** (s)	[moldavsko]

Monaco	**Monako** (s)	[monako]
Mongolia	**Mongolsko** (s)	[mongolsko]
Montenegro	**Černá Hora** (ž)	[ʧɛrnaː hora]

| Morocco | **Maroko** (s) | [maroko] |
| Myanmar | **Barma** (ž) | [barma] |

Namibia	**Namibie** (ž)	[namɪbɪe]
Nepal	**Nepál** (m)	[nɛpaːl]
Netherlands	**Nizozemí** (s)	[nɪzozɛmiː]
New Zealand	**Nový Zéland** (m)	[novi zɛːlant]
North Korea	**Severní Korea** (ž)	[severni korɛa]
Norway	**Norsko** (s)	[norsko]

101. Countries. Part 3

Pakistan	Pákistán (m)	[paːkɪstaːn]
Palestine	Palestinská autonomie (ž)	[palɛstɪnska: autonomɪe]
Panama	Panama (ž)	[panama]
Paraguay	Paraguay (ž)	[paragvaj]
Peru	Peru (s)	[pɛru]
Poland	Polsko (s)	[polsko]
Portugal	Portugalsko (s)	[portugalsko]
Romania	Rumunsko (s)	[rumunsko]
Russia	Rusko (s)	[rusko]
Saudi Arabia	Saúdská Arábie (ž)	[sau:dska: ara:bɪe]
Scotland	Skotsko (s)	[skotsko]
Senegal	Senegal (m)	[sɛnɛgal]
Serbia	Srbsko (s)	[srpsko]
Slovakia	Slovensko (s)	[slovɛnsko]
Slovenia	Slovinsko (s)	[slovɪnsko]
South Africa	Jihoafrická republika (ž)	[jɪhoafrɪtska: rɛpublɪka]
South Korea	Jižní Korea (ž)	[jɪʒni: korɛa]
Spain	Španělsko (s)	[ʃpanelsko]
Suriname	Surinam (m)	[surɪnam]
Sweden	Švédsko (s)	[ʃvɛ:tsko]
Switzerland	Švýcarsko (s)	[ʃvi:tsarsko]
Syria	Sýrie (ž)	[si:rɪe]
Taiwan	Tchaj-wan (m)	[tajvan]
Tajikistan	Tádžikistán (m)	[ta:dʒɪkɪsta:n]
Tanzania	Tanzanie (ž)	[tanzanɪe]
Tasmania	Tasmánie (ž)	[tasma:nɪe]
Thailand	Thajsko (s)	[tajsko]
Tunisia	Tunisko (s)	[tunɪsko]
Turkey	Turecko (s)	[turɛtsko]
Turkmenistan	Turkmenistán (m)	[turkmɛnɪsta:n]
Ukraine	Ukrajina (ž)	[ukrajɪna]
United Arab Emirates	Spojené arabské emiráty (m mn)	[spojɛnɛ: arapskɛ: ɛmɪra:tɪ]
United States of America	Spojené státy (m mn) americké	[spojɛnɛ: sta:tɪ amɛrɪtskɛ:]
Uruguay	Uruguay (ž)	[urugvaj]
Uzbekistan	Uzbekistán (m)	[uzbɛkɪsta:n]
Vatican	Vatikán (m)	[vatɪka:n]
Venezuela	Venezuela (ž)	[vɛnɛzuɛla]
Vietnam	Vietnam (m)	[vjɛtnam]
Zanzibar	Zanzibar (m)	[zanzɪbar]

GASTRONOMIC GLOSSARY

This section contains a lot of
words and terms associated
with food. This dictionary will
make it easier for you to
understand the menu at a
restaurant and choose
the right dish

T&P Books Publishing

aftertaste	příchuť (ž)	[prʃiːxutʲ]
almond	mandle (ž)	[mandlɛ]
anise	anýz (m)	[aniːz]
aperitif	aperitiv (m)	[apɛrɪtɪf]
appetite	chuť (ž) k jídlu	[xutʲ k jiːdlu]
appetizer	předkrm (m)	[prʃɛtkrm]
apple	jablko (s)	[jablko]
apricot	meruňka (ž)	[mɛrunʲka]
artichoke	artyčok (m)	[artɪtʃok]
asparagus	chřest (m)	[xrʃɛst]
Atlantic salmon	losos (m)	[losos]
avocado	avokádo (s)	[avokaːdo]
bacon	slanina (ž)	[slanɪna]
banana	banán (m)	[banaːn]
barley	ječmen (m)	[jɛtʃmɛn]
bartender	barman (m)	[barman]
basil	bazalka (ž)	[bazalka]
bay leaf	bobkový list (m)	[bopkoviː lɪst]
beans	boby (m mn)	[bobɪ]
beef	hovězí (s)	[hoveziː]
beer	pivo (s)	[pɪvo]
beet	červená řepa (ž)	[tʃɛrvenaː rʒɛpa]
bell pepper	pepř (m)	[pɛprʃ]
berries	bobule (ž mn)	[bobulɛ]
berry	bobule (ž)	[bobulɛ]
bilberry	borůvky (ž mn)	[boruːfkɪ]
birch bolete	kozák (m)	[kozaːk]
bitter	hořký	[horʃkiː]
black coffee	černá káva (ž)	[tʃɛrna kaːva]
black pepper	černý pepř (m)	[tʃɛrniː pɛprʃ]
black tea	černý čaj (m)	[tʃɛrniː tʃaj]
blackberry	ostružiny (ž mn)	[ostruʒɪnɪ]
blackcurrant	černý rybíz (m)	[tʃɛrniː rɪbiːz]
boiled	vařený	[varʒɛniː]
bottle opener	otvírač (m) lahví	[otviːratʃ lahviː]
bread	chléb (m)	[xlɛːp]
breakfast	snídaně (ž)	[sniːdane]
bream	cejn (m)	[tsɛjn]
broccoli	brokolice (ž)	[brokolɪtsɛ]
Brussels sprouts	růžičková kapusta (ž)	[ruːʒɪtʃkova kapusta]
buckwheat	pohanka (ž)	[pohaŋka]
butter	máslo (s)	[maːslo]
buttercream	krém (m)	[krɛːm]
cabbage	zelí (s)	[zɛliː]

cake	zákusek (m)	[zaːkusɛk]
cake	dort (m)	[dort]
calorie	kalorie (ž)	[kalorɪe]
can opener	otvírač (m) konzerv	[otviːratʃ konzɛrf]
candy	bonbón (m)	[bonboːn]
canned food	konzerva (ž)	[konzɛrva]
cappuccino	kapučíno (s)	[kaputʃiːno]
caraway	kmín (m)	[kmiːn]
carbohydrates	karbohydráty (mn)	[karbohɪdratiː]
carbonated	perlivý	[pɛrlɪviː]
carp	kapr (m)	[kapr]
carrot	mrkev (ž)	[mrkɛf]
catfish	sumec (m)	[sumɛts]
cauliflower	květák (m)	[kvetaːk]
caviar	kaviár (m)	[kavɪaːr]
celery	celer (m)	[tsɛlɛr]
cep	hřib (m)	[hrʒɪp]
cereal crops	obilniny (ž mn)	[obɪlnɪnɪ]
champagne	šampaňské (s)	[ʃampanʲskɛː]
chanterelle	liška (ž)	[lɪʃka]
check	účet (m)	[uːtʃɛt]
cheese	sýr (m)	[siːr]
chewing gum	žvýkačka (ž)	[ʒviːkatʃka]
chicken	slepice (ž)	[slɛpɪtsɛ]
chocolate	čokoláda (ž)	[tʃokolaːda]
chocolate	čokoládový	[tʃokolaːdoviː]
cinnamon	skořice (ž)	[skorʒɪtsɛ]
clear soup	vývar (m)	[viːvar]
cloves	hřebíček (m)	[hrʒɛbiːtʃɛk]
cocktail	koktail (m)	[koktajl]
coconut	kokos (m)	[kokos]
cod	treska (ž)	[trɛska]
coffee	káva (ž)	[kaːva]
coffee with milk	bílá káva (ž)	[biːlaː kaːva]
cognac	koňak (m)	[konʲak]
cold	studený	[studɛniː]
condensed milk	kondenzované mléko (s)	[kondɛnzovanɛː mlɛːko]
condiment	ochucovadlo (s)	[oxutsovadlo]
confectionery	cukroví (s)	[tsukroviː]
cookies	sušenky (ž mn)	[suʃɛŋkɪ]
coriander	koriandr (m)	[korɪandr]
corkscrew	vývrtka (ž)	[viːvrtka]
corn	kukuřice (ž)	[kukurʒɪtsɛ]
corn	kukuřice (ž)	[kukurʒɪtsɛ]
cornflakes	kukuřičné vločky (ž mn)	[kukurʒɪtʃnɛː vlotʃkɪ]
course, dish	jídlo (s)	[jiːdlo]
cowberry	brusinky (ž mn)	[brusɪŋkɪ]
crab	krab (m)	[krap]
cranberry	klikva (ž)	[klɪkva]
cream	sladká smetana (ž)	[slatkaː smɛtana]
crumb	drobek (m)	[drobɛk]
crustaceans	korýši (m mn)	[koriːʃɪ]

cucumber	okurka (ž)	[okurka]
cuisine	kuchyně (ž)	[kuxɪne]
cup	šálek (m)	[ʃaːlɛk]
dark beer	tmavé pivo (s)	[tmavɛ: pɪvo]
date	datle (ž)	[datlɛ]
death cap	prašivka (ž)	[praʃɪfka]
dessert	desert (m)	[dɛsɛrt]
diet	dieta (ž)	[dɪeta]
dill	kopr (m)	[kopr]
dinner	večeře (ž)	[vɛtʃɛrʒɛ]
dried	sušený	[suʃɛni:]
drinking water	pitná voda (ž)	[pɪtna: voda]
duck	kachna (ž)	[kaxna]
ear	klas (m)	[klas]
edible mushroom	jedlá houba (ž)	[jɛdla: houba]
eel	úhoř (m)	[u:horʃ]
egg	vejce (s)	[vɛjtsɛ]
egg white	bílek (m)	[bi:lɛk]
egg yolk	žloutek (m)	[ʒloutɛk]
eggplant	lilek (m)	[lɪlɛk]
eggs	vejce (s mn)	[vɛjtsɛ]
Enjoy your meal!	Dobrou chuť!	[dobrou xutʲ]
fats	tuky (m)	[tukɪ]
fig	fík (m)	[fi:k]
filling	nádivka (ž)	[na:dɪfka]
fish	ryby (ž mn)	[rɪbɪ]
flatfish	platýs (m)	[plati:s]
flour	mouka (ž)	[mouka]
fly agaric	muchomůrka (ž) červená	[muxomu:rka tʃɛrvɛna:]
food	jídlo (s)	[ji:dlo]
fork	vidlička (ž)	[vɪdlɪtʃka]
freshly squeezed juice	vymačkaná šťáva (ž)	[vɪmatʃkana: ʃtʲaːva]
fried	smažený	[smaʒeni:]
fried eggs	míchaná vejce (s mn)	[mi:xana: vɛjtsɛ]
frozen	zmražený	[zmraʒeni:]
fruit	ovoce (s)	[ovotsɛ]
fruits	ovoce (s mn)	[ovotsɛ]
game	zvěřina (ž)	[zverʒɪna]
gammon	kýta (ž)	[ki:ta]
garlic	česnek (m)	[tʃɛsnɛk]
gin	džin (m)	[dʒɪn]
ginger	zázvor (m)	[za:zvor]
glass	sklenice (ž)	[sklɛnɪtsɛ]
glass	sklenka (ž)	[sklɛŋka]
goose	husa (ž)	[husa]
gooseberry	angrešt (m)	[angrɛʃt]
grain	obilí (s)	[obɪli:]
grape	hroznové víno (s)	[hroznovɛ: vi:no]
grapefruit	grapefruit (m)	[grɛjpfru:t]
green tea	zelený čaj (m)	[zɛlɛni: tʃaj]
greens	zelenina (ž)	[zɛlɛnɪna]
groats	kroupy (ž mn)	[kroupɪ]

halibut	platýs (m)	[plati:s]
ham	šunka (ž)	[ʃuŋka]
hamburger	mleté maso (s)	[mlɛtɛ: maso]
hamburger	hamburger (m)	[hamburgɛr]
hazelnut	lískový ořech (m)	[li:skovi: orʒɛx]
herring	sleď (ž)	[slɛtʲ]
honey	med (m)	[mɛt]
horseradish	křen (m)	[krʃɛn]
hot	teplý	[tɛpli:]
ice	led (m)	[lɛt]
ice-cream	zmrzlina (ž)	[zmrzlɪna]
instant coffee	rozpustná káva (ž)	[rozpustna: ka:va]
jam	džem (m)	[dʒem]
jam	zavařenina (ž)	[zavarʒɛnɪna]
juice	šťáva (ž), džus (m)	[ʃtʲa:va], [dʒus]
kidney bean	fazole (ž)	[fazolɛ]
kiwi	kiwi (s)	[kɪvɪ]
knife	nůž (m)	[nu:ʃ]
lamb	skopové (s)	[skopovɛ:]
lemon	citrón (m)	[tsɪtro:n]
lemonade	limonáda (ž)	[lɪmona:da]
lentil	čočka (ž)	[tʃotʃka]
lettuce	salát (m)	[sala:t]
light beer	světlé pivo (s)	[svetlɛ: pɪvo]
liqueur	likér (m)	[lɪkɛ:r]
liquors	alkoholické nápoje (m mn)	[alkoholɪtskɛ: na:pojɛ]
liver	játra (s mn)	[ja:tra]
lunch	oběd (m)	[obet]
mackerel	makrela (ž)	[makrɛla]
mandarin	mandarinka (ž)	[mandarɪŋka]
mango	mango (s)	[mango]
margarine	margarín (m)	[margari:n]
marmalade	marmeláda (ž)	[marmɛla:da]
mashed potatoes	bramborová kaše (ž)	[bramborova: kaʃɛ]
mayonnaise	majonéza (ž)	[majonɛ:za]
meat	maso (s)	[maso]
melon	cukrový meloun (m)	[tsukrovi: mɛloun]
menu	jídelní lístek (m)	[ji:dɛlni: li:stɛk]
milk	mléko (s)	[mlɛ:ko]
milkshake	mléčný koktail (m)	[mlɛtʃni: koktajl]
millet	jáhly (ž mn)	[ja:hlɪ]
mineral water	minerální voda (ž)	[mɪnɛra:lni: voda]
morel	smrž (m)	[smrʃ]
mushroom	houba (ž)	[houba]
mustard	hořčice (ž)	[horʃtʃɪtsɛ]
non-alcoholic	nealkoholický	[nɛalkoholɪtski:]
noodles	nudle (ž mn)	[nudlɛ]
oats	oves (m)	[ovɛs]
olive oil	olivový olej (m)	[olɪvovi: olɛj]
olives	olivy (ž)	[olɪvɪ]
omelet	omeleta (ž)	[omɛlɛta]
onion	cibule (ž)	[tsɪbulɛ]

orange	pomeranč (m)	[pomɛrantʃ]
orange juice	pomerančový džus (m)	[pomɛrantʃovi: dʒus]
orange-cap boletus	křemenáč (m)	[krʃɛmɛna:tʃ]
oyster	ústřice (ž)	[u:strʃɪtsɛ]
pâté	paštika (ž)	[paʃtɪka]
papaya	papája (ž)	[papa:ja]
paprika	paprika (ž)	[paprɪka]
parsley	petržel (ž)	[pɛtrʒel]
pasta	makaróny (m mn)	[makaro:nɪ]
pea	hrách (m)	[hra:x]
peach	broskev (ž)	[broskɛf]
peanut	burský oříšek (m)	[burski: orʒi:ʃɛk]
pear	hruška (ž)	[hruʃka]
peel	slupka (ž)	[slupka]
perch	okoun (m)	[okoun]
pickled	marinovaný	[marɪnovani:]
pie	koláč (m)	[kola:tʃ]
piece	kousek (m)	[kousɛk]
pike	štika (ž)	[ʃtɪka]
pike perch	candát (m)	[tsanda:t]
pineapple	ananas (m)	[ananas]
pistachios	pistácie (ž)	[pɪsta:tsɪe]
pizza	pizza (ž)	[pɪtsa]
plate	talíř (m)	[tali:rʃ]
plum	švestka (ž)	[ʃvɛstka]
poisonous mushroom	jedovatá houba (ž)	[jɛdovata: houba]
pomegranate	granátové jablko (s)	[grana:tovɛ: jablko]
pork	vepřové (s)	[vɛprʃovɛ:]
porridge	kaše (ž)	[kaʃɛ]
portion	porce (ž)	[portsɛ]
potato	brambory (ž mn)	[bramborɪ]
proteins	bílkoviny (ž)	[bi:lkovɪnɪ]
pub, bar	bar (m)	[bar]
pudding	pudink (m)	[pudɪŋk]
pumpkin	tykev (ž)	[tɪkɛf]
rabbit	králík (m)	[kra:li:k]
radish	ředkvička (ž)	[rʒɛtkvɪtʃka]
raisin	hrozinky (ž mn)	[hrozɪŋkɪ]
raspberry	maliny (ž mn)	[malɪnɪ]
recipe	recept (m)	[rɛtsɛpt]
red pepper	červená paprika (ž)	[tʃɛrvɛna: paprɪka]
red wine	červené víno (s)	[tʃɛrvɛnɛ: vi:no]
redcurrant	červený rybíz (m)	[tʃɛrvɛni: rɪbi:z]
refreshing drink	osvěžující nápoj (m)	[osvɛʒuji:tsi: na:poj]
rice	rýže (ž)	[ri:ʒe]
rum	rum (m)	[rum]
russula	holubinka (ž)	[holubɪŋka]
rye	žito (s)	[ʒɪto]
saffron	šafrán (m)	[ʃafra:n]
salad	salát (m)	[sala:t]
salmon	losos (m)	[losos]
salt	sůl (ž)	[su:l]

salty	slaný	[slani:]
sandwich	obložený chlebíček (m)	[oblozeni: xlɛbi:tʃɛk]
sardine	sardinka (ž)	[sardɪŋka]
sauce	omáčka (ž)	[oma:tʃka]
saucer	talířek (m)	[tali:rʒɛk]
sausage	salám (m)	[sala:m]
seafood	mořské plody (m mn)	[morʃkɛ: plodɪ]
sesame	sezam (m)	[sɛzam]
shark	žralok (m)	[ʒralok]
shrimp	kreveta (ž)	[krɛvɛta]
side dish	příloha (ž)	[prʃi:loha]
slice	plátek (m)	[pla:tɛk]
smoked	uzený	[uzɛni:]
soft drink	nealkoholický nápoj (m)	[nɛalkoholɪtski: na:poj]
soup	polévka (ž)	[polɛ:fka]
soup spoon	polévková lžíce (ž)	[polɛ:fkova: ɮi:tsɛ]
sour cherry	višně (ž)	[vɪʃne]
sour cream	kyselá smetana (ž)	[kɪsɛla: smɛtana]
soy	sója (ž)	[so:ja]
spaghetti	spagety (m mn)	[spagɛtɪ]
sparkling	perlivý	[pɛrlɪvi:]
spice	koření (s)	[korʒɛni:]
spinach	špenát (m)	[ʃpɛna:t]
spiny lobster	langusta (ž)	[langusta]
spoon	lžíce (ž)	[ɮi:tsɛ]
squid	sépie (ž)	[sɛ:pɪe]
steak	biftek (m)	[bɪftɛk]
still	neperlivý	[nɛpɛrlɪvi:]
strawberry	zahradní jahody (ž mn)	[zahradni: jahodɪ]
sturgeon	jeseter (m)	[jɛsɛtɛr]
sugar	cukr (m)	[tsukr]
sunflower oil	slunečnicový olej (m)	[slunɛtʃnɪtsovi: olɛj]
sweet	sladký	[slatki:]
sweet cherry	třešně (ž)	[trʃɛʃne]
taste, flavor	chuť (ž)	[xutʲ]
tasty	chutný	[xutni:]
tea	čaj (m)	[tʃaj]
teaspoon	kávová lžička (ž)	[ka:vova: ɮɪtʃka]
tip	spropitné (s)	[spropɪtnɛ:]
tomato	rajské jablíčko (s)	[rajskɛ: jabli:tʃko]
tomato juice	rajčatová šťáva (ž)	[rajtʃatova: ʃtʲa:va]
tongue	jazyk (m)	[jazɪk]
toothpick	párátko (s)	[pa:ra:tko]
trout	pstruh (m)	[pstrux]
tuna	tuňák (m)	[tunʲa:k]
turkey	krůta (ž)	[kru:ta]
turnip	vodní řepa (ž)	[vodni: rʒɛpa]
veal	telecí (s)	[tɛlɛtsi:]
vegetable oil	olej (m)	[olɛj]
vegetables	zelenina (ž)	[zɛlɛnɪna]
vegetarian	vegetarián (m)	[vɛgɛtarɪa:n]
vegetarian	vegetariánský	[vɛgɛtarɪa:nski:]

vermouth	vermut (m)	[vɛrmut]
vienna sausage	párek (m)	[paːrɛk]
vinegar	ocet (m)	[otsɛt]
vitamin	vitamín (m)	[vɪtamiːn]
vodka	vodka (ž)	[votka]
wafers	oplatky (mn)	[oplatkɪ]
waiter	číšník (m)	[tʃiːʃniːk]
waitress	číšnice (ž)	[tʃiːʃnɪtsɛ]
walnut	vlašský ořech (m)	[vlaʃski: orʒɛx]
water	voda (ž)	[voda]
watermelon	vodní meloun (m)	[vodni: mɛloun]
wheat	pšenice (ž)	[pʃɛnɪtsɛ]
whiskey	whisky (ž)	[vɪskɪ]
white wine	bílé víno (s)	[biːlɛ: viːno]
wild strawberry	jahody (ž mn)	[jahodɪ]
wine	víno (s)	[viːno]
wine list	nápojový lístek (m)	[naːpojoviː liːstɛk]
with ice	s ledem	[s lɛdɛm]
yogurt	jogurt (m)	[jogurt]
zucchini	cukina, cuketa (ž)	[tsukɪna], [tsuketa]

Czech-English gastronomic glossary

účet (m)	[uːʧɛt]	check
úhoř (m)	[uːhorʃ]	eel
ústřice (ž)	[uːstrʃɪtsɛ]	oyster
číšník (m)	[ʧiːʃniːk]	waiter
číšnice (ž)	[ʧiːʃnɪtsɛ]	waitress
čaj (m)	[ʧaj]	tea
černá káva (ž)	[ʧɛrna: kaːva]	black coffee
černý čaj (m)	[ʧɛrniː ʧaj]	black tea
černý pepř (m)	[ʧɛrni: pɛprʃ]	black pepper
černý rybíz (m)	[ʧɛrni: rɪbiːz]	blackcurrant
červená řepa (ž)	[ʧɛrvena: rʒɛpa]	beet
červená paprika (ž)	[ʧɛrvɛna: paprɪka]	red pepper
červené víno (s)	[ʧɛrvɛnɛ: viːno]	red wine
červený rybíz (m)	[ʧɛrvɛni: rɪbiːz]	redcurrant
česnek (m)	[ʧɛsnɛk]	garlic
čočka (ž)	[ʧoʧka]	lentil
čokoláda (ž)	[ʧokolaːda]	chocolate
čokoládový	[ʧokolaːdovi:]	chocolate
ředkvička (ž)	[rʒɛtkvɪʧka]	radish
šálek (m)	[ʃaːlɛk]	cup
šťáva (ž), džus (m)	[ʃtʲaːva], [dʒus]	juice
šafrán (m)	[ʃafraːn]	saffron
šampaňské (s)	[ʃampanʲskɛ:]	champagne
špenát (m)	[ʃpɛnaːt]	spinach
štika (ž)	[ʃtɪka]	pike
šunka (ž)	[ʃuŋka]	ham
švestka (ž)	[ʃvɛstka]	plum
žito (s)	[ʒɪto]	rye
žloutek (m)	[ʒloutɛk]	egg yolk
žralok (m)	[ʒralok]	shark
žvýkačka (ž)	[ʒviːkaʧka]	chewing gum
alkoholické nápoje (m mn)	[alkoholɪtskɛ: naːpojɛ]	liquors
anýz (m)	[ani:z]	anise
ananas (m)	[ananas]	pineapple
angrešt (m)	[angrɛʃt]	gooseberry
aperitiv (m)	[apɛrɪtɪf]	aperitif
artyčok (m)	[artɪʧok]	artichoke
avokádo (s)	[avoka:do]	avocado
bílá káva (ž)	[bi:la: ka:va]	coffee with milk
bílé víno (s)	[bi:lɛ: vi:no]	white wine
bílek (m)	[bi:lɛk]	egg white
bílkoviny (ž)	[bi:lkovɪnɪ]	proteins
banán (m)	[bana:n]	banana
bar (m)	[bar]	pub, bar

barman (m)	[barman]	bartender
bazalka (ž)	[bazalka]	basil
biftek (m)	[bɪftɛk]	steak
bobkový list (m)	[bopkovi: lɪst]	bay leaf
bobule (ž mn)	[bobulɛ]	berries
bobule (ž)	[bobulɛ]	berry
boby (m mn)	[bobɪ]	beans
bonbón (m)	[bonbo:n]	candy
borůvky (ž mn)	[boru:fkɪ]	bilberry
bramborová kaše (ž)	[bramborova: kaʃɛ]	mashed potatoes
brambory (ž mn)	[bramborɪ]	potato
brokolice (ž)	[brokolɪtsɛ]	broccoli
broskev (ž)	[broskɛf]	peach
brusinky (ž mn)	[brusɪŋkɪ]	cowberry
burský oříšek (m)	[burski: orʒi:ʃɛk]	peanut
candát (m)	[tsanda:t]	pike perch
cejn (m)	[tsɛjn]	bream
celer (m)	[tsɛlɛr]	celery
chřest (m)	[xrʃɛst]	asparagus
chléb (m)	[xlɛ:p]	bread
chuť (ž)	[xutʲ]	taste, flavor
chuť (ž) k jídlu	[xutʲ k ji:dlu]	appetite
chutný	[xutni:]	tasty
cibule (ž)	[tsɪbulɛ]	onion
citrón (m)	[tsɪtro:n]	lemon
cukina, cuketa (ž)	[tsukɪna], [tsuketa]	zucchini
cukr (m)	[tsukr]	sugar
cukroví (s)	[tsukrovi:]	confectionery
cukrový meloun (m)	[tsukrovi: mɛloun]	melon
džem (m)	[dʒem]	jam
džin (m)	[dʒɪn]	gin
datle (ž)	[datlɛ]	date
desert (m)	[dɛsɛrt]	dessert
dieta (ž)	[dɪeta]	diet
Dobrou chuť!	[dobrou xutʲ]	Enjoy your meal!
dort (m)	[dort]	cake
drobek (m)	[drobɛk]	crumb
fík (m)	[fi:k]	fig
fazole (ž)	[fazolɛ]	kidney bean
granátové jablko (s)	[grana:tovɛ: jablko]	pomegranate
grapefruit (m)	[grɛjpfru:t]	grapefruit
hřebíček (m)	[hrʒɛbi:tʃɛk]	cloves
hřib (m)	[hrʒɪp]	cep
hamburger (m)	[hamburgɛr]	hamburger
hořčice (ž)	[horʃtʃɪtsɛ]	mustard
hořký	[horʃki:]	bitter
holubinka (ž)	[holubɪŋka]	russula
houba (ž)	[houba]	mushroom
hovězí (s)	[hovezi:]	beef
hrách (m)	[hra:x]	pea
hrozinky (ž mn)	[hrozɪŋkɪ]	raisin
hroznové víno (s)	[hroznovɛ: vi:no]	grape

hruška (ž)	[hruʃka]	pear
husa (ž)	[husa]	goose
jáhly (ž mn)	[ja:hlɪ]	millet
játra (s mn)	[ja:tra]	liver
jídelní lístek (m)	[ji:dɛlni: li:stɛk]	menu
jídlo (s)	[ji:dlo]	course, dish
jídlo (s)	[ji:dlo]	food
jablko (s)	[jablko]	apple
jahody (ž mn)	[jahodɪ]	wild strawberry
jazyk (m)	[jazɪk]	tongue
ječmen (m)	[jɛtʃmɛn]	barley
jedlá houba (ž)	[jɛdla: houba]	edible mushroom
jedovatá houba (ž)	[jɛdovata: houba]	poisonous mushroom
jeseter (m)	[jɛsɛtɛr]	sturgeon
jogurt (m)	[jogurt]	yogurt
káva (ž)	[ka:va]	coffee
kávová lžička (ž)	[ka:vova: ʒɪtʃka]	teaspoon
kýta (ž)	[ki:ta]	gammon
křemenáč (m)	[krʃɛmɛna:tʃ]	orange-cap boletus
křen (m)	[krʃɛn]	horseradish
kaše (ž)	[kaʃɛ]	porridge
kachna (ž)	[kaxna]	duck
kalorie (ž)	[kalorɪe]	calorie
kapr (m)	[kapr]	carp
kapučíno (s)	[kaputʃi:no]	cappuccino
karbohydráty (mn)	[karbohɪdrati:]	carbohydrates
kaviár (m)	[kavɪa:r]	caviar
kiwi (s)	[kɪvɪ]	kiwi
klas (m)	[klas]	ear
klikva (ž)	[klɪkva]	cranberry
kmín (m)	[kmi:n]	caraway
koňak (m)	[konʲak]	cognac
koření (s)	[korʒɛni:]	spice
kokos (m)	[kokos]	coconut
koktail (m)	[koktajl]	cocktail
koláč (m)	[kola:tʃ]	pie
kondenzované mléko (s)	[kondɛnzovanɛ: mlɛ:ko]	condensed milk
konzerva (ž)	[konzɛrva]	canned food
kopr (m)	[kopr]	dill
korýši (m mn)	[kori:ʃɪ]	crustaceans
koriandr (m)	[korɪandr]	coriander
kousek (m)	[kousɛk]	piece
kozák (m)	[koza:k]	birch bolete
králík (m)	[kra:li:k]	rabbit
krém (m)	[krɛ:m]	buttercream
krůta (ž)	[kru:ta]	turkey
krab (m)	[krap]	crab
kreveta (ž)	[krɛvɛta]	shrimp
kroupy (ž mn)	[kroupɪ]	groats
kuchyně (ž)	[kuxɪne]	cuisine
kukuřičné vločky (ž mn)	[kukurʒɪtʃnɛ: vlotʃkɪ]	cornflakes
kukuřice (ž)	[kukurʒɪtsɛ]	corn

kukuřice (ž)	[kukurʒɪtsɛ]	corn
květák (m)	[kveta:k]	cauliflower
kyselá smetana (ž)	[kɪsɛla: smɛtana]	sour cream
lískový ořech (m)	[li:skovi: orʒɛx]	hazelnut
lžíce (ž)	[lʒi:tsɛ]	spoon
langusta (ž)	[langusta]	spiny lobster
led (m)	[lɛt]	ice
liška (ž)	[lɪʃka]	chanterelle
likér (m)	[lɪkɛ:r]	liqueur
lilek (m)	[lɪlɛk]	eggplant
limonáda (ž)	[lɪmona:da]	lemonade
losos (m)	[losos]	salmon
losos (m)	[losos]	Atlantic salmon
máslo (s)	[ma:slo]	butter
míchaná vejce (s mn)	[mi:xana: vɛjtsɛ]	fried eggs
majonéza (ž)	[majonɛ:za]	mayonnaise
makaróny (m mn)	[makaro:nɪ]	pasta
makrela (ž)	[makrɛla]	mackerel
maliny (ž mn)	[malɪnɪ]	raspberry
mandarinka (ž)	[mandarɪŋka]	mandarin
mandle (ž)	[mandlɛ]	almond
mango (s)	[mango]	mango
margarín (m)	[margari:n]	margarine
marinovaný	[marɪnovani:]	pickled
marmeláda (ž)	[marmɛla:da]	marmalade
maso (s)	[maso]	meat
med (m)	[mɛt]	honey
meruňka (ž)	[mɛrunʲka]	apricot
minerální voda (ž)	[mɪnɛra:lni: voda]	mineral water
mléčný koktail (m)	[mlɛtʃni: koktajl]	milkshake
mléko (s)	[mlɛ:ko]	milk
mleté maso (s)	[mlɛtɛ: maso]	hamburger
mořské plody (m mn)	[morʃskɛ: plodɪ]	seafood
mouka (ž)	[mouka]	flour
mrkev (ž)	[mrkɛf]	carrot
muchomůrka (ž) červená	[muxomu:rka tʃɛrvɛna:]	fly agaric
nádivka (ž)	[na:dɪfka]	filling
nápojový lístek (m)	[na:pojovi: li:stɛk]	wine list
nůž (m)	[nu:ʃ]	knife
nealkoholický	[nɛalkoholɪtski:]	non-alcoholic
nealkoholický nápoj (m)	[nɛalkoholɪtski: na:poj]	soft drink
neperlivý	[nɛpɛrlɪvi:]	still
nudle (ž mn)	[nudlɛ]	noodles
oběd (m)	[obet]	lunch
obilí (s)	[obɪli:]	grain
obilniny (ž mn)	[obɪlnɪnɪ]	cereal crops
obložený chlebíček (m)	[obloʒeni: xlɛbi:tʃɛk]	sandwich
ocet (m)	[otsɛt]	vinegar
ochucovadlo (s)	[oxutsovadlo]	condiment
okoun (m)	[okoun]	perch
okurka (ž)	[okurka]	cucumber
olej (m)	[olɛj]	vegetable oil

olivový olej (m)	[olɪvovi: olɛj]	olive oil
olivy (ž)	[olɪvɪ]	olives
omáčka (ž)	[oma:tʃka]	sauce
omeleta (ž)	[omɛlɛta]	omelet
oplatky (mn)	[oplatkɪ]	wafers
ostružiny (ž mn)	[ostruʒɪnɪ]	blackberry
osvěžující nápoj (m)	[osveʒuji:tsi: na:poj]	refreshing drink
otvírač (m) konzerv	[otvi:ratʃ konzɛrf]	can opener
otvírač (m) lahví	[otvi:ratʃ lahvi:]	bottle opener
oves (m)	[ovɛs]	oats
ovoce (s mn)	[ovotsɛ]	fruits
ovoce (s)	[ovotsɛ]	fruit
párátko (s)	[pa:ra:tko]	toothpick
párek (m)	[pa:rɛk]	vienna sausage
příchuť (ž)	[prʃi:xutʲ]	aftertaste
příloha (ž)	[prʃi:loha]	side dish
předkrm (m)	[prʃɛtkrm]	appetizer
pšenice (ž)	[pʃɛnɪtsɛ]	wheat
paštika (ž)	[paʃtɪka]	pâté
papája (ž)	[papa:ja]	papaya
paprika (ž)	[paprɪka]	paprika
pepř (m)	[pɛprʃ]	bell pepper
perlivý	[pɛrlɪvi:]	carbonated
perlivý	[pɛrlɪvi:]	sparkling
petržel (ž)	[pɛtrʒel]	parsley
pistácie (ž)	[pɪsta:tsɪe]	pistachios
pitná voda (ž)	[pɪtna: voda]	drinking water
pivo (s)	[pɪvo]	beer
pizza (ž)	[pɪtsa]	pizza
plátek (m)	[pla:tɛk]	slice
platýs (m)	[plati:s]	halibut
platýs (m)	[plati:s]	flatfish
pohanka (ž)	[pohaŋka]	buckwheat
polévka (ž)	[polɛ:fka]	soup
polévková lžíce (ž)	[polɛ:fkova: ɮʒi:tsɛ]	soup spoon
pomeranč (m)	[pomɛrantʃ]	orange
pomerančový džus (m)	[pomɛrantʃovi: dʒus]	orange juice
porce (ž)	[portsɛ]	portion
prašivka (ž)	[praʃɪfka]	death cap
pstruh (m)	[pstrux]	trout
pudink (m)	[pudɪŋk]	pudding
rýže (ž)	[ri:ʒe]	rice
růžičková kapusta (ž)	[ru:ʒɪtʃkova: kapusta]	Brussels sprouts
rajčatová šťáva (ž)	[rajtʃatova: ʃtʲa:va]	tomato juice
rajské jablíčko (s)	[rajskɛ: jabli:tʃko]	tomato
recept (m)	[rɛtsɛpt]	recipe
rozpustná káva (ž)	[rozpustna: ka:va]	instant coffee
rum (m)	[rum]	rum
ryby (ž mn)	[rɪbɪ]	fish
s ledem	[s lɛdɛm]	with ice
sépie (ž)	[sɛ:pɪe]	squid
sója (ž)	[so:ja]	soy

sýr (m)	[si:r]	cheese
sůl (ž)	[su:l]	salt
salám (m)	[sala:m]	sausage
salát (m)	[sala:t]	lettuce
salát (m)	[sala:t]	salad
sardinka (ž)	[sardɪŋka]	sardine
sezam (m)	[sɛzam]	sesame
sklenice (ž)	[sklɛnɪtsɛ]	glass
sklenka (ž)	[sklɛŋka]	glass
skořice (ž)	[skorʒɪtsɛ]	cinnamon
skopové (s)	[skopovɛ:]	lamb
sladká smetana (ž)	[slatka: smɛtana]	cream
sladký	[slatki:]	sweet
slaný	[slani:]	salty
slanina (ž)	[slanɪna]	bacon
sleď (ž)	[slɛtʲ]	herring
slepice (ž)	[slɛpɪtsɛ]	chicken
slunečnicový olej (m)	[slunɛtʃnɪtsovi: olɛj]	sunflower oil
slupka (ž)	[slupka]	peel
smažený	[smaʒeni:]	fried
smrž (m)	[smrʃ]	morel
snídaně (ž)	[sni:dane]	breakfast
spagety (m mn)	[spagɛtɪ]	spaghetti
spropitné (s)	[spropɪtnɛ:]	tip
studený	[studɛni:]	cold
sušený	[suʃɛni:]	dried
sušenky (ž mn)	[suʃɛŋkɪ]	cookies
sumec (m)	[sumɛts]	catfish
světlé pivo (s)	[svetlɛ: pɪvo]	light beer
třešně (ž)	[trʃɛʃne]	sweet cherry
talíř (m)	[tali:rʃ]	plate
talířek (m)	[tali:rʒɛk]	saucer
telecí (s)	[tɛlɛtsi:]	veal
teplý	[tɛpli:]	hot
tmavé pivo (s)	[tmavɛ: pɪvo]	dark beer
treska (ž)	[trɛska]	cod
tuňák (m)	[tunʲa:k]	tuna
tuky (m)	[tukɪ]	fats
tykev (ž)	[tɪkɛf]	pumpkin
uzený	[uzɛni:]	smoked
víno (s)	[vi:no]	wine
vývar (m)	[vi:var]	clear soup
vývrtka (ž)	[vi:vrtka]	corkscrew
vařený	[varʒeni:]	boiled
večeře (ž)	[vɛtʃɛrʒɛ]	dinner
vegetarián (m)	[vɛgɛtarɪa:n]	vegetarian
vegetariánský	[vɛgɛtarɪa:nski:]	vegetarian
vejce (s mn)	[vɛjtsɛ]	eggs
vejce (s)	[vɛjtsɛ]	egg
vepřové (s)	[vɛprʃovɛ:]	pork
vermut (m)	[vɛrmut]	vermouth
višně (ž)	[vɪʃne]	sour cherry

vidlička (ž)	[vɪdlɪtʃka]	fork
vitamín (m)	[vɪtami:n]	vitamin
vlašský ořech (m)	[vlaʃski: orʒɛx]	walnut
voda (ž)	[voda]	water
vodka (ž)	[votka]	vodka
vodní řepa (ž)	[vodni: rʒɛpa]	turnip
vodní meloun (m)	[vodni: mɛloun]	watermelon
vymačkaná šťáva (ž)	[vɪmatʃkana: ʃtʲa:va]	freshly squeezed juice
whisky (ž)	[vɪskɪ]	whiskey
zákusek (m)	[za:kusɛk]	cake
zázvor (m)	[za:zvor]	ginger
zahradní jahody (ž mn)	[zahradni: jahodɪ]	strawberry
zavařenina (ž)	[zavarʒɛnɪna]	jam
zelí (s)	[zɛli:]	cabbage
zelený čaj (m)	[zɛlɛni: tʃaj]	green tea
zelenina (ž)	[zɛlɛnɪna]	vegetables
zelenina (ž)	[zɛlɛnɪna]	greens
zmražený	[zmraʒeni:]	frozen
zmrzlina (ž)	[zmrzlɪna]	ice-cream
zvěřina (ž)	[zverʒɪna]	game